SELL
LIKE
CRAZY

SABRI SUBY

Creator: Suby, Sabri

Title: Sell Like Crazy: How To Get As Many Clients, Customers and Sales As You Can Possibly Handle

ISBN:

978-0-6484599-0-3 (paper back)

978-0-6484599-2-7 (ebook)

978-0-6484599-1-0 (audio book)

Disclaimer

The advice provided in this publication is general advice only. It has been prepared without taking into account your objectives, financial situation or business needs. Before acting on this advice you should consider the appropriateness of the advice, having regard to your own objectives, financial situation and business needs. To the maximum extent permitted by law, the author and publisher disclaim all responsibility and liability to any person, arising directly or indirectly from any person taking or not taking action based on the information in this publication.

Printed in Australia by McPherson's Printing Group

To my mother, who raised me with the belief that anything is possible and encouraged me to chase my dreams.

To my wife and our daughter Melia. Without your unwavering support, sacrifice, and belief in me, this work would not be possible.

Contents

IMPORTANT!
READ THIS FIRST!

Dear Friend,

Your decision to purchase this book may turn out to be the smartest decision you've ever made.

As you are about to learn, this book totally delivers on every promise I've made in my advertising.

Not only that, every sales-boosting idea you're about to read has been tested and proven to work in almost every industry on the planet. From dentists to dog walkers, property investment to pizza delivery, this selling system works.

These ideas have already generated hundreds of millions of dollars in revenue for my clients and me.

The simple secrets you will learn in Phase 1 have generated more than $1.33 billion in the 416 different industries and niches I've deployed them in.

And this: The amazing secret in Phase 2 that can make your advertising pull 300% more leads and sales off each and every ad.

And this: The #1 best way to grab any reader by the jugular... and pull them into your sales message... and... almost force them to buy! This is one of my biggest and most powerful secrets. (Even some of the biggest digital marketers in the world don't know this core concept.) Phase 3 reveals all…

And this: The secrets revealed in Phase 3 are the very same ones I used to help explode the sales of a home-building startup from $0 to $7million in under 8 months.

And this: The secrets revealed in Phase 4 are the very same ones I used to help Raphael Bender multiply the sales of his Pilates instructor training company, Breathe Education, by more than 500% in just 12 months!

And this: The secrets revealed in Phase 4 will allow you to turn every advertising dollar into $2, $3, or $4, and outspend all your competitors… leaving them dumbfounded!

And this: The secrets in the other phases should remove almost every roadblock that has ever stopped you from exploding the sales of your business!

These strategies aren't restricted to big companies with huge marketing budgets. I've used this secret selling system to generate hundreds of millions of dollars in sales for businesses of all sizes.

It's an immensely powerful system because of four core reasons:

- IT WORKS FAST. Unlike traditional advertising, which takes months of preparation and a long time to see results, this selling system can be ready to go in a few weeks for immediate, trackable results.

- IT'S CHEAP. The businesses successfully using this system have, in many cases, not spent a single cent more on their marketing budgets.

- IT'S TIMELESS. This isn't one of your trendy online marketing gimmicks that relies on hacks and workarounds. It's a strategy that's worked for decades and will continue to work for a long time to come.

- IT SCALES. This selling system works for any size business, from a sole trader all the way up to a billion-dollar company. And its success isn't about how much money you throw at it, but how well you do it.

Before I begin, there's something you need *to understand first*:

It will not be easy. It will take hard work and dedication from YOU. It will require you to believe 100% in your product or service, and it will require you to back that belief with a measurable financial investment to market it to the world.

If you think you can become a millionaire overnight, or get floods of orders by spending $200 a month on advertising, then this book isn't right for you.

In fact, and I honestly mean no offence when I say this, I don't even want you to read this book! You won't get anything out of it. There are no silver bullets, hacks, or gimmicks here, so you'd only be wasting your time. I suggest you stop reading now and return the book to where you got it for a refund

I know this sounds strange – I mean, what author in their right mind would urge people not to read their book?

What you need to understand is how passionate I am and how seriously I take this. If you're not 100% committed to throwing everything you have behind the success of your business, then I can't help you. For me, as with everything else in life, it's all or nothing.

However, if you are ready to commit and go all in, in the following pages you'll discover a selling system that will truly bring you a predictable, reliable, and consistent flow of new customers.

Now listen: Somewhere down the line, you're going to realise the information in this book is worth hundreds of thousands, if not millions of dollars. And you're going to start wondering why I'm revealing all these inside secrets for such a low price.

The reason is rather simple. You see, I run a very successful digital agency called King Kong. And we have the privilege of working with a handful of billion-dollar companies and hundreds of small-to-medium size businesses to dramatically grow their sales.

The thing is, almost every week I receive emails and handwritten letters from business owners who can't afford our services but desperately need help with growing their business. Up until now, I haven't been able to meet their needs.

Then I had an idea! Instead of sending them to the numbskulls who are rampant in the advertising industry, especially in agencies, I put together this playbook on the best sales-producing strategies known to man, with the exact steps on how to grow the sales of any business and sell like crazy!

This is my way of giving back to a community that has made all my wildest dreams possible. No matter where you are on your journey, I hope this book dramatically helps you.

I want to thank you for giving me this chance to prove myself to you.

Sincerely,

Sabri Suby

P.S. You will benefit more if you read this book straight through from cover to cover instead of 'hopping around' from one section to another.

Ready? Let's get started!

Why This Information Is Vitally Important – Now More Than Ever

The statistics are grim: 96% of all businesses fail within 10 years, with 80% failing within the first two years. But even the 4% that make it aren't necessarily successful or profitable; it just means they've survived.

If this weren't enough… 95% of companies will never reach $1 million in annual sales.

And out of these rare few, 95% won't ever make it to $5 million.

And of those, 98% won't get to $10 million. And very, very few go beyond $100 million.

Why do so few businesses grow and become profitable? I'll tell you: The difference is the dedication and drive of the company's leaders to sharpen and apply the skills that matter. And the number one skill is being able to produce revenue.

In simple terms, this is being able to ring the cash register in large enough volumes with high enough margins to sustain and grow the business.

Repeated, profitable sales are the lifeblood of your business. The oxygen. Without them, your business will die.

If you have the ability to grow your revenue profitably, there's almost no business problem you can't solve.

You see, most businesses are started by the 'practitioner' – that is, the artist trying to turn his or her art into a business.

Take the chef who starts a catering business because they love to cook. Nowhere has this chef been given the tools and education to run a successful business. They likely went to cooking school or did an apprenticeship.

Maybe, if they were lucky enough, there was one unit of study that included something about running your own business. The problem? The course material was likely put together by someone who had never run or scaled a successful business!

Yet this chef is meant to know how to run a business, how to acquire customers, and differentiate themselves from the hundreds of other businesses that all claim to do the same thing.

Along the way, they try to figure out all this 'sales and marketing stuff', while juggling the pressures of heading into the unknown and running a start-up company.

What's the difference between a chef who starts a catering business and 20 years later realises they've created a job, not a business, and another who starts a catering business and in 10 years has 16 locations and then sells it for a multi-million-dollar pay day? The difference isn't in the food; it's in the marketing and selling of that food.

This book gives you the exact learning curve and selling system I've used to take fledgling start-ups and turn them into multi-million-dollar businesses – businesses where the founder has been pulling 80-hour weeks, been up at night, tossing and turning, worried where his or her next customer is coming from. After implementing this secret selling system in their business, they've gone from breakeven and barely drawing a wage to a thriving multi-million-dollar business, all while reducing their workload by up to 60%.

In other words, going from working 80 hours per week down to 32 and making 700% more money.

By the way, I haven't implemented this amazing system in only a handful of businesses so I could then tout it as the 'holy grail' of business growth.

I've personally implemented this into *thousands* of businesses and have advised *tens of thousands* on how to implement it themselves.

In the process, I've run thousands of scientific advertising split tests to find out what works and what doesn't.

In short, I've used these systems and strategies to add hundreds of millions of dollars of revenue to businesses of all types and sizes.

All these hard-won secrets are included in this book.

Think Like A Billionaire

If you want to *become* a billionaire, you need to *think* like a billionaire.

Just to be clear, by 'billionaire' I mean *self-made* billionaire. Not the person with the massive inherited wealth they did nothing to earn. I'm talking about the person *just like you*, who started out with very little. The person who had to work for a living.

To think like a self-made billionaire, you must first understand their choices in life and in business. Where do they derive their income from? What do they spend their time on? What tasks do they focus on? In short, what do they *invest* themselves in?

I have obsessively studied this unique group of high achievers. I've found **they invest only in assets that provide a positive return.**

There are many kinds of assets. Among billionaires, the most valuable, non-renewable asset in the world is their time.

So how do billionaires spend their most valuable asset – their precious time?

Are they constantly checking emails, posting on social media, doing Facebook Live streams and other low-level activities they could delegate to a team member or outsource?

The answer should be obvious.

Many billionaires don't even use email or a mobile phone, and some go off the grid for weeks at a time. How is this possible in the 21st century, especially when building billion-dollar empires in the technology age?

Take well-known billionaire John Paul DeJoria. He's the founder of tequila maker Patrón Spirits Co., and cofounder of hair care company John Paul Mitchell Systems.

He slept in his car and sold shampoo door-to-door before teaming up with Paul Mitchell in 1980 and turning $700 into John Paul Mitchell Systems, a company that currently does a billion dollars in annual sales.

Having recently sold his 70% stake in Patrón Spirits Co. for $5.1 billion, DeJoria is now worth an estimated $3.4 billion.

He famously doesn't have an email address, and chooses to streamline all communications by not using email… *ever.*

This powerhouse managed to build not one, but two billion-dollar businesses without ever using email or owning a smartphone.

DeJoria lives a very tech-minimal lifestyle. While he drives a Tesla, you won't ever find a computer, laptop, or tablet in his possession. And it's all for a valid reason: 'I'd be inundated if I did email', he says.

Because the truth is, the more successful you get, it's what you say 'no' to that makes the difference. Meaning billionaires look at how they can take more off their plate and invest their time in the activities that really move the needle.

Am I saying you should give away all your material possessions and do away with technology forever? No.

I am, however, making the point that hitting refresh on your email to see if the world is coming to an end every 15 minutes is living life in a *reactive state*. It doesn't allow you to invest your time into deep work that produces revenue.

Take Mark Ford, for example. Since 1993 he's been the chief growth strategist for Agora Inc., the direct response information marketing behemoth with revenues heading north of a billion dollars.

Ford went from $100,000 in debt to a net worth of $240 million, and says one of the biggest reasons why most businesses never lift off is because of an obsession with 'little chores'.

Little chores are things that keep you busy but don't make you any money… or even worse, lose you money.

Instead of working on important tasks, most business owners let the squeakiest wheel get the grease. They waste time on low-yielding tasks that earn them a minimum return, like constantly checking emails and activities they could delegate or outsource. Meanwhile, they forgo the activities that produce the bulk of the revenue for their business – what I like to call **Highly Leveraged Activities.**

Let me ask you a question, and be honest: Does your business suffer from the following symptoms?

- Do you wonder where your next client is going to come from?

- Are you overwhelmed and overworked with trivial activities?

- Are you not focussing on high-yielding, revenue-producing activities?

- Are you trading time for money and not earning your true value?

- Are you stuck in a state of feast or famine?

- Are competitors with inferior products and services seeing more success than you and stealing your market share?

If you answered 'yes' to any of the above, then you're likely so busy working 'in' your business in a reactive state that you never get time to work 'on' your business – and you're making a fatal mistake.

Now compare that type of business to a successful, thriving business grounded in a lead and revenue-producing system like I'm going to show you in this book. A wildly successful business is a business where:

- Customers chase you, and not the other way around.

- Predictability and consistency generate new leads, clients, and revenue.

- You speak only to highly-qualified prospects you can actually help.

- You have an automated lead-generation system that delivers new customers on demand with minimal human effort.

- You focus only on the Highly Leveraged Activities that produce revenue.

So, here's the bottom line: Being busy is not the same as being productive. Our lives are full of distractions, and it's hard to stay focussed when your world consists of hundreds of tiny tasks and millions of voices screaming for your attention.

As the founder of a business that you're looking to scale, your focus needs to move from doing the everyday work to producing revenue for your business and steering the ship.

If you don't aspire to scale your business and you're content with simply practising your craft, that's fine; however, this book likely isn't for you. The selling system outlined in this book is for business owners hungry for growth.

You see, just like the chef we spoke of above, the money in business isn't in your product or service, it's in the **selling of your product or service.**

What I mean is, no matter what industry you're in, once you've got a few team members, and you're looking to scale your business, you're no longer a builder, baker, or business consultant. **You're a marketer.**

The fate of your business lies not just in having the best product or service but in your ability to *market* your products or services. While this might be difficult for you to accept, it's true.

I'm not saying you don't want to have the best product or service in your industry, I'm saying the money is not *in* that – because if you can't effectively communicate that to your market, it doesn't matter.

The market doesn't pay you to have the best products or service. It rewards you for *solving problems*. A transaction takes places where, in the mind of the consumer, the value of the solution you're selling outweighs the price you're asking.

In other words, you'll be compensated on the basis of how you market and build value around your solution to the pains and desires of your customers.

The bigger the problem you solve, the more you will be compensated.

Your focus should be on intimately understanding your market and your prospects' deepest desires, pains, fears, hopes, and dreams. You need to know them better than any of your competitors, and then craft marketing messages that effectively communicate how you can solve these problems.

This exercise is the single most valuable activity you can do in your business.

I refer to these Highly Leveraged Activities as the 4% of activities that move the money needle. In reality, 20% of activities bring in 80% of your company's revenue.

The 4% Rule For Moving The Money Needle

This really became clear to me when I learned about Vilfredo Pareto.

Pareto was an Italian economist who became famous for his 80/20 rule. This is now commonly called the Pareto principle.

He first discovered this rule when he found that 80% of a nation's wealth was controlled by 20% of the population. As he studied this phenomenon more deeply, he found a disproportionate relationship between cause and effect in other areas of life, including real estate, growing crops, and all sorts of things:

20% of the input creates 80% of the result.

20% of the workers produce 80% of the result.

20% of the customers create 80% of the revenue.

20% of the roads cause 80% of the crashes.

And on and on...

In my deep dives into marketing psychology, I've found

his 80/20 rule to hold true for almost all areas of business, including...

- Popularity of products.

- Sources of incoming leads.

- Customer service problems.

- Reasons customers buy.

- Activities in your business that produce revenue!

And while you might have heard about the 80/20 rule, most people never truly apply it to their business let alone other areas of their life.

In business, the little stuff kills the big stuff. What I mean is that there are lots of small, nit-picky things in your business constantly screaming for attention, but these aren't the tasks that produce revenue.

When I started to apply this in my business, revenue skyrocketed. To give you an example, here are my business activities:

All Business Activities

- Checking emails
- Writing copy
- Speaking with clients
- Having meetings
- Creating Facebook ads
- Checking stats
- Creating systems & processes
- Coming up with offers & promotions
- Training/On-boarding staff

- Creating sales funnels
- Sending emails
- Shooting videos
- Recruiting
- Running errands
- Making webinars
- Creating proposals
- Scheming & plotting
- Setting up systems
- Looking at analytics
- Public relations/ Interviews

The 80/20 rule demonstrates you can and should disregard 80% of your business activities. They should either be delegated or outsourced so you can focus on the top 20% that produce revenue.

Once you've done this in your business, you need to take it one step further and truly become a high-performance entrepreneur. You see, you should apply the 80/20 rule to the 80/20 rule itself. That is to say, 80% of the 80% of the revenue comes from 20% of the 20% of your revenue-producing activities.

To put it more simply…

4% of your activities create 64% of the revenue in your business

In my business, after cutting out the 96% of my activities that produced little or no revenue, this is what the top 4% revenue-producing activities looked like:

Revenue-Producing Activities

- Writing sales copy
- Coming up with offers & promotions
- Creating sales funnels
- Shooting videos
- Doing webinars
- Scheming & plotting

Because these 4% of activities literally bring in 64% of all the revenue for my business, I hired an operations manager and other team leaders to do all the other things that don't move the money needle.

Sadly, here is where most entrepreneurs and top employees mess up. Instead of investing their time exclusively in their super-productive 4%, too many business owners and salespeople get caught up in the minutiae of the day-to-day 96%. All day long, they go from putting out one fire to another, never having a chance to invest time working on the 4% that moves the money needle and propels their business forward.

So what are your top 4% revenue-producing activities?

Are they creating new offers? Motivating sales staff? Increasing lifetime customer value? Whatever it is, you need to figure it out.

And once you've put together a list of these vitally important revenue-producing activities, it's time to get to work and start automating and creating systems for just about everything else.

You shouldn't invest your time in boring, low-value tasks. Because every minute you spend on low-value tasks or putting out fires is time taken away from the areas of your business that have the most leverage and the largest potential to make you money.

This goes well beyond business activities. You see, you want to audit your time and where it is being spent and where you are getting the most leverage. For example, are you still cleaning your house, cooking your meals, doing laundry, and running errands?

This life admin work is nothing more than a collection of low-level activities that can easily be outsourced. But how do you know when it's time to hire a cook or a cleaner?

The very first step is to figure out how much you're earning per hour right now.

Value Of Your Current Time

I work____hours per week and I make $_____per week. _____hours ÷ $_____ = hourly rate

Once you have figured out how much your hourly rate is, you don't want to complete any tasks that you could hire someone to do for a lesser rate. Let's say you make $3,000 per week and work 40 hours, resulting in your hourly rate being $75 per hour.

You can hire a cook or cleaner for $20 per hour to free up more of your time to work on your business. You do it. Immediately. Because it's not costing you $20 per hour to clean your house or to have your meals cooked, it's saving you $55 per hour.

That's right, if you were to do those tasks yourself, you would be actually losing $55 per hour, if not a lot more. This is because if you clean your house for an hour, you're not able to earn your rate of $75 per hour. You're essentially hiring yourself at $20 per hour when you could hire yourself at $75 per hour.

Download and complete The King's Audit worksheet to get a better understanding of where you should be spending your time.

Remember my 4% rule.

Only 4% of your activities each day drive your business forward and move the money needle. The other 96% of the things still have to get done, but they shouldn't get done by you.

Action Points

- Download 'The King's Audit' worksheet at: https://resources.selllikecrazy.co/

- Make a list of all of your business activities.

- Conduct an 80/20 analysis of these activities.

- Create an action plan to help you delegate, automate or outsource the 80% of your activities that don't produce revenue or move your business forward.

- Then take it one step further and invest your time only in the 4% of activities that bring in the most revenue.

How To Sell Like Crazy

Let me be brutally clear and not mince my words about what I believe to be the single most important rule in business.

It is this:

As the owner, your number one responsibility is to *sell*.

Selling is not something you do on the side. It's not something you can outsource or completely delegate. It's the single most important job of any business and consequently any founder or owner.

It doesn't matter whether you have a great product or service… Your entire existence as an entrepreneur lives and dies by how effective your sales and marketing is at producing new revenue.

Your business success is *not* based on your motivation, your team, your passion, or your desire to help people.

If you have a marketing and sales machine that predictably brings in hordes of new customers every day like clockwork, owning a business can be phenomenal.

If you don't, owning a business can be unpredictable, unreliable, and incredibly stressful. This is because the destiny of your company, your income, your family's income, and the income of your employees and their families rest in whatever 'fate' drops in your lap.

You can choose to ignore this fact, turn a blind eye, and tell yourself that 'everything will work out fine'. Or you can read this book from cover to cover and ensure your business doesn't become a depressing statistic.

Either way, you must understand that all the latest shiny marketing tactics, hacks and tools being peddled will not solve the number one problem business owners face: 'How do I get more customers – and therefore more revenue?'

More tactics are not the answer. And you likely already know this deep down inside. Because if you're like most business owners, you've gone through countless CRM software programs, landing page builders, all the latest gizmos and gadgets and you may have even hired marketing agencies, only to find very little success.

The reason for this is because these are all designed to treat the symptoms to low sales and not cure the systemic cause of the problem.

You need something different.

Are You Ready?

In this book, I'm going to tell you things you won't hear anywhere else. The methods I divulge in the following pages are highly controversial.

Not because they're untrue. It's because they are truer than anything else you've likely ever been taught about sales and marketing.

What you'll discover in this book is going to change everything for you, and especially the way you think about business and your income.

You see, after working with thousands of business owners and entrepreneurs, I've realised most business owners don't really understand the business they are in.

What I mean is the baker thinks they are in the baking business, the builder thinks they are in the building business, and the dentist thinks they are in the dentistry business.

When in fact they are not.

They are in the business of selling those particular products and services.

You bake bread. You build homes. You fill cavities. This part of your business, the product or service, is likely the reason you got started in business, and it's easy to get wrapped up in this kind of thinking: 'I'm a builder, so I must spend my time building homes'.

The fact is, most of the business owner's time should be spent on the real business that every business owner is in – selling.

As a business owner, selling should be your number one priority – and you must act accordingly. This means spending the bulk of your time on marketing and sales-related activities – or as I call them, *revenue-producing activities.*

This doesn't mean you have to be the one on the phone actually doing the selling yourself. Nor does it mean you must write every piece of sales copy on your website. However, you must be very much involved in every step of the sales and marketing process, so you understand the problems intimately and can identify the opportunities.

Because it doesn't matter what sort of expertise you bring to your business – whether you're a problem solver, a great manager, a numbers person, or a systems and processes person.

To be a truly effective entrepreneur, you must become your business's number one expert at selling.

There is only one way to do this, and that is to invest most of your time, attention and energy in revenue producing activities – or the activity of selling.

The ratio of time, effort and money spent on selling as opposed to other aspects of business should be 80/20, with 80% of it going toward revenue-producing activities and only 20% towards all the other management activities in your business. Or, if you have a team in place, you should apply this 80/20 analysis again, and only be focussed on your 4% of activities that move the money needle.

You see, there are five major functions of business—product development, customer service, accounting, operations, and marketing.

The one function that should always be given top priority in any business is marketing.

The other functions are clearly vital to a well-functioning business, yet without marketing you will not have sales and without sales, you will not have cash flow and without cash flow your business will die from lack of cash, which is the oxygen to any business. Without it you will not be able to pay for all the other functions, and you will go out of business very quickly.

Sales Trumps All

I believe this to be the number one rule in business. Sales trumps all.

Sales are the 'tip of the spear', and everything else stems from this point.

I hope by this point I've convinced you that, as the business owner, selling should be your primary job.

I've seen this to be true from working with thousands of clients in countless businesses of all different types, sizes, and industries. Establishing a selling system like the one outlined in this book is up to 90% of the battle in running a wildly successful business.

Because if your business is being flooded with profitable sales, there really is no problem you can't solve with the right amount of money. No one you can't hire. No system you can't implement.

Selling is not an optional task for an entrepreneur – it's essential. And if selling is essential, then *learning* to sell (i.e., developing the knowledge and skills needed to sell) is an obligation, not a choice.

In this Phase, I will show you how to become a master at selling. Don't worry if you don't know anything about selling yet. Everything you're about to learn is easy to follow, and I'll teach you the lessons I've learned from years in the trenches.

But first…

Why Should You Listen To A Single Word I Have To Say?

Great question.

Let me preface this by explaining that the following information hasn't been learned simply by sitting around philosophising on the subject of sales, reading books, attending sales seminars, or watching YouTube videos.

No.

I've spent seventeen long years in the trenches, on the front lines 'doing the work'. Collecting battle scars to find out every secret sales technique in existence.

If there was a rumour of a technique, even on the other side of the world, I hunted it down. If there was some hot shot claiming to be a master salesman in some god-forsaken corner of the earth, I found them.

If there was so much as a whisper of a selling secret ANYWHERE, I tested it.

In my years as a sales professional, I've studied every book, course, method, and video I could find.

But I was never satisfied with what I found because the truth is that...

99% of what you hear consists of outdated, pushy sales tactics that work only on unsophisticated prospects – and definitely wouldn't work in today's fast-changing digital economy.

These are hard-won lessons I've collected like battle scars from the trenches and the front lines.

I am a master salesperson, and with my proven process, even the best salespeople in the world find it hard to compete with me. Let me explain where it all started…

Single Parent Mother Work Ethic

I grew up in a small regional beach town in northern New South Wales, Australia, called Byron Bay. It has a population of 9,000.

My older sister and I were raised by a single mother. I watched my mother hold down three jobs and work tirelessly to give us a great life.

She would wake up before the sun and go to work before we left for school, and she would often get home after we did. She would then head straight to the kitchen to cook us a healthy dinner. As exhausted as she was, she did all this with a smile and the affection and warmth only a loving mother can provide.

There were times that were rough, and we had no money. Yet she always found a way to pull through.

When I was eight years old, I started waking up early so I could help her set up the café where she worked before I went to school. I would sweep the floor, take out the tables and chairs, and set them up. When I was finished, she would give me a hot chocolate and some breakfast as my 'reward'. Afterwards, kissing me on the cheek, she'd tell me she loved me and send me off to school.

Why am I telling you all this? Far out, isn't this meant to be a book about marketing?

Yes, but this is an important point.

Watching my mother work so hard to provide a great upbringing for my sister and me taught me the most valuable lesson I've ever learned.

And that is this: Nothing in life comes without hard work. Nothing is given to you. You don't get what you 'deserve'. You get what you push, shove, scratch, and work your ass off for. My mother taught me firsthand that having a strong work ethic is the number one determining factor for success.

After seeing this, I wanted to pull my own weight to help her. So, still only eight years old, I got my first weekend job – making peanut butter at the local health food store for $2.50 per hour. I would give all the money I made to her.

However, I soon realised that even if I worked eight hours a day, I would never be able to make a contribution that made my mother's life easier.

So I got to thinking – how can I make more money to help out my mum? I found an old harmonica and decided to busk at the Sunday markets. I had no idea what I was doing or even how to play the harmonica, yet this didn't stop me.

I threw my baseball cap on the ground, pulled out my harmonica, and started playing. I'll never forget that first day I made $80 in five hours. It would have taken me thirty-two hours making peanut butter at the health food store to earn that much!

I ran home eagerly to show my mum, but when I tried to give it to her, she insisted I keep it for myself. I refused and she burst into tears, gave me a big hug, and squeezed me tight.

I knew from her tears this money would make an impact and actually help her out. I didn't mind whether it would go towards the electricity bill or the weekly groceries, I just wanted to help. I worked every Sunday market from that point on, switching up my busking acts from harmonica to juggling.

Little did I know at the time what a valuable lesson I was learning, and that this single parent mother work ethic would serve me well the rest of my life.

At sixteen, I got my first full-time job in sales. I'll never forget it. The job ad in the local paper said, 'Earn up to $1800 per week. No experience required'. I was sold.

It was a group interview of 30, and I got the job along with two other candidates. We joined a team of 13 others, all crammed into an office, converted from an old shipping container. We were tasked with making 100 cold calls an hour – calling so fast we could hardly put the phone back on the hook. Feverishly, we worked our way through call sheets of businesses. I still remember the sound of production in that shipping container – it was deafening.

We were calling businesses to buy back their empty ink cartridges and then selling them back refilled. I was making 600 cold calls a day, being abused, hung-up on, and yelled at. People were screaming at me, 'Fuck off little kid', or 'Go fucking die!' It was a cold hard slap in the face. Here I was at the front lines of capitalism, and I was getting bruised and bloody from the rejection.

Worst of all, I was failing miserably.

After two weeks, my production was well below the other rookies. It seemed I was the runt of the litter. I had my review with the owner who liked me and said even though I was performing terribly, he wanted to give me another seven days to see if I could turn things around.

After I stepped out of that meeting and went home for the day, I thought long and hard about what I was doing and why I wasn't being successful. I said to myself, 'Fuck it', and it was as if it flicked a switch inside of me. Whether it was the owner seeing some promise and taking a chance on me, or me being backed into a corner knowing it was all on the line, I don't know – maybe it was a combination of both – but something fundamentally changed that day.

I started looking at sales as a game. I would run through walls to get to a 'yes' from a prospect. Objections would bounce off me like bullets to Batman. Overnight I literally became the company's top producer. I couldn't be stopped.

This success led me to seek out and study the greatest orators and communicators of all time. I started to examine human psychology and the art of persuasion. I applied what I was learning, refining my pitch, seeing what worked and what didn't. If I changed my tone and cadence here or there, how would it affect my success rate?

I became unstoppable. I was 17 and making close to $2,000 per week. It was this early success that got me thinking about travelling the world to seek more opportunities than my small hometown could provide.

After high school, while most of my friends were moving to Sydney or Melbourne for university, I decided it wasn't for me. So I packed my bags and moved to London to start my adventures.

I would continue to work in sales, selling everything you can imagine over the phone, from telecommunications, satellite TV, mobile payment devices, and even legal will writing.

I worked at companies with sales floors jam-packed

with 2,000 people, and other companies with smaller, more involved sales teams. From multi-billion-dollar corporations to start-ups and everything in between.

I was the top salesperson at every company I ever worked at, for every month that I worked there. A fresh-faced kid from Byron Bay, not only holding his own in one of the world's financial epicentres, but beating the pants off everyone.

How?

Well, I would like to say I was born with it. Some innate and natural talent. 'He's a natural salesman', people would say.

That isn't the case.

The answer is an unrivalled work ethic and hunger to master my craft, learned from watching my mum slave away, raise two children, and wear the responsibilities of two parents, all with a smile on her face.

I coined this quality the 'single parent mother work ethic'. My personal motto was:

I don't care how talented you are, how fortunate your upbringing was, or even if you had a better education or opportunities than me. You simply can't outwork me. Ever.

And it's this principle that continues to serve me. When I started King Kong in 2014 from my bedroom – with no money, no venture capital, and no safety net – I was entering a market with incredibly established players who had deep pockets and a huge head start. But over the intervening years I've made many of these competitors wave the white flag and surrender. I've sent a lot of these companies either out of business or I've forced their hand to sell, as they simply can't keep up with the fire-breathing marketing machine that is King Kong.

This principle still serves me today. I start my days at 4am, hungry for success, always willing to put the work in to make my dreams a reality.

And it's something I suggest you instil and forge in yourself. Because all the strategies and tactics in this book, or anywhere else, won't mean anything if you don't *put in the work.*

Your work ethic is the only thing you can control in life.

And if you strengthen it, stretch it to its limit, and forge an unrivalled work ethic that burns inside of you, you will win.

Having a single parent mother work ethic means being relentless. It means demanding more of yourself than anyone else could ever demand of you, knowing that every time you get tired, you can still do more.

Put. In. The. Work. Every. Day. Do something you don't want to do first thing every morning. Challenge yourself to be uncomfortable and push past the mediocre, the laziness, and the fear. Forge your work ethic and exercise it like a muscle. Strengthen it. Build it. Be relentless in your approach towards success.

No marketing hack, sales funnel, or software can make you successful if you're not going to do the work. Don't wait for someone to make it happen for you. It's on you. And that's why I'm telling you all of this, not because I want you to know how hard I work, but because I want you to know what you have to do for yourself to be successful in whatever path you choose in life.

I'm not here to sugarcoat life. I'm not here to coddle you or tell you what you want to hear. Nor am I here to paint a picture of a lavish laptop lifestyle by the beach, sipping piña coladas as you click 'refresh' on your internet banking account. Is that attainable? Yes. Does it require a crap-load more work than the Instagram famous would have you believe? Yes.

But most people don't talk about it. They would rather show you their rented Lamborghini on Instagram. Or how they did a million-dollar week, all through affiliates and joint ventures, hiding all the painstaking work that goes into something like that. Or living their life as a façade on social media, trying to sell you their system on how you can 'click a button to riches', just like the false reality they're living.

Sorry, not me. Not in this book. I'm going to tell you what you need to hear.

I'm here to cut the bullshit and kick-start the life and business you were meant to have so that you can reach your fullest potential as an entrepreneur and ultimately fuel every other area of your life.

Discipline, structure, rules, rituals, planning. These are the frameworks for success, yet these are not attractive things in today's world of instant gratification. The average person reaches for the latest hack or loophole to attaining success with the least amount of work possible. However, that is a fool's errand and will leave you broke.

Wherever you are now, however hard you're working, I want you to take it to another level you didn't even know was even possible. Get into that zone where you can shut out all the noise, negativity, fear, distractions, and lies, and achieve all that you want in whatever you do. I want you to light a fire inside yourself so big and so ablaze that no one can deny you.

In business and in life, there are a multitude of factors outside of your control: How well funded your competitors are, the size and experience of their team, when they got started in business, their joint venture partners... All of these things are outside of your control.

The thing that is within your control is how hard you work. In anything you do, to work hard takes no special talent, luck, or exceptional resources. You simply just have to be willing to put in the work and do it.

There are no excuses. It's no one else's fault. It's all on you.

You must be completely focussed on taking full ownership and responsibility for every bit of success and every bit of failure that comes your way. Decide how to get the job done and then do whatever is necessary to make it happen.

When you make a mistake, don't look for excuses. Don't blame other people. Own it. 100%.

Kill The 'Little Bitch' Inside

Strong words, I know. But let me explain. Anytime you've had an internal struggle over what you want to do, versus what you know you should do... that's the Little Bitch inside you're wrestling with.

It may be when your alarm goes off and the voice inside your head says, 'You've been working hard and had a late night – just hit snooze and take another ten minutes. You need it. You deserve it. Close your eyes and just rest'. That's the Little Bitch whispering in your ear. If your Little Bitch is strong, it probably gets you to hit that snooze button of death several times before getting out of bed.

Or maybe your Little Bitch rears its ugly head and tries to convince you to miss a workout, going on to justify and sell you on all the reasons why it's ok to skip a session: 'You're still sore from yesterday's session, and you've been consistent all week, just take a rest day today – it's all good'. Again – that's the Little Bitch.

Or how about when you're at the office taking care of business? It might be when you're calling potential candidates to join your team, replying to emails, or writing sales copy for a new offer. Perhaps you're making sales calls and the Little Bitch comes out and whispers, 'You've already had a bunch of great calls today with a handful of hopefuls, so don't worry about following up and calling every last proposal you sent last week. You're doing great. And hey, if they're really interested in buying, they'll call you'. Little Bitch again.

This duality of human nature exists in all of us. I call this character the Little Bitch because it's always pulling at your heels, putting weight and resistance on you as you're trying to make a better life for yourself. It's looking out only for its best interest!

We all have one, living inside, whether it's incredibly vocal or dormant and lingering, only rearing its head in testing times. It's there. Living and breathing. Testing you. Forging your will. Seeing how bad you want it.

You need willpower, which is the control exerted to either do something or restrain impulses and the ability to control your own thoughts.

If you're required to exert willpower to do something, it means there's internal conflict. It means, the 'why' is not big enough or the 'why' hasn't overtaken your desire for whatever the alternative is.

You want to make your 'why' so big that your 'how' becomes easy.

Your self-control is what will distinguish you from all the others. It's what will give you the ability to show up every day, whether it's at the gym, at school, building your business, making money, or training in martial arts. It's doing what no one else is willing to do, so you can achieve what they won't. That's what comes from conquering your Little Bitch and forging your self-control and discipline.

You know what I'm talking about and you probably can't believe I'm talking about it. But I am. You not only need to come to terms with its existence, but also with the fact that you have to get it under control.

You must let the Little Bitch know who's in control. Let it know who's the master. Starve it of oxygen and never let it see the light of day. Remove all the fear and inhibition it breeds. You must let your hunger for success, in all areas of your life, out-wrestle your Little Bitch, making it obedient to your hunger for success.

Without this deep hunger for success, it's like trying to work a lighter that has no fuel. You get sputtering little sparks, maybe even a short-lived flame, but no fire.

Your hunger and drive must be blazing so big, so bright, and so furious that no one can deny it. You must crave success so intensely that the work it takes to attain it is irrelevant.

Fall in love with the work itself, not just the result. Learn to enjoy the excruciating pain, you must endure to be successful. Success isn't just talent. Talent will help get you started but it won't get you to the Promised Land. You have to create a work ethic that ensures you become successful. Hard work and effort will beat talent 99% of the time. Put in the work to ensure your success. Don't look for shortcuts. Don't make excuses.

People are always asking me about the secrets and growth hacks I use to grow businesses. Sorry if this disappoints you, but there are no secrets. Yes, there are strategies, tactics, and levers you can pull to unlock serious growth in your business – however, they all require you to put in the work to make them work.

The only qualification that I would add is you have to work hard on what *gets results*. Invest your time in the 4% that drives cash flow. Love the work itself, but set goals and demand results from yourself. Plan for progress and achieve it.

Instead of looking for get-rich-quick-schemes, secrets, hacks, magic pills, or silver bullets, roll up your sleeves and get ready to do the work.

Take an honest look at where you are now and where you want to be. Then, ask yourself what you're willing to do to get there. What fire are you willing to walk through? How much pain are you willing to tolerate? Then make a plan to get there, act on it, and do whatever it takes.

Your job is to be the best entrepreneur and business person you can be. To do that you have to train and practise to master your craft, continually learning and getting better at the activities that really move the needle for your business.

You want to train and level-up your abilities as much as you can, as often as you can. So, I want you to imagine this scenario:

There is one business owner who wakes up at 8am, has breakfast and gets to work at 9:30am, answers emails, manages some admin, and begins to work on important activities by 11am. One hour of work goes by, and it's 12pm – time for lunch. He goes to lunch and is back in the office at 1:30pm. There are a few emails that need replying to, and after doing that it's now 2:30pm. His focus turns back to the important activities, and it takes fifteen minutes to get back in the zone and start to focus. An hour goes by and it's 3:45pm when the phone rings. He gets stuck on a call with a client, vendor, or manager. By the time he finishes, it's 4:30pm. A few more emails have come through, along with a handful of messages on office chat. It's now 5:30pm and time to go home and 'switch off' for the day.

Add it up: over the entire day, his actual productive time spent creating value for himself and his company was two hours.

Now imagine another entrepreneur who wakes up at 4am. He heads to the gym, listening to an audiobook on his 30-minute commute, levelling-up and feeding his brain with new information. He completes a 45-minute workout, then a sauna session to get in peak state keeping the mind sharp for the day ahead. He showers and heads to the office, again listening to an audiobook, gaining insights, arriving at the office at 7am. He dives straight into deep work on the activities that really matter. No checking emails, no distractions, just laser-like focus on the task at hand. 9am comes around, two hours have flown by as he's been in a deep, focussed and uninterrupted state. He stops for 20 minutes to have a packed breakfast and grab a coffee.

It's now 9:20am, and he's back at his desk, jumping straight back into deep work on highly-leveraged activities that will move the business forward. Another two hours go by, it's 11:20am. He hops inside his inbox, archiving and deleting emails that don't need a reply, actioning others with short, sharp responses, or simply jumping on the phone for two minutes to sort out an issue that would take 20 minutes to deal with via email. By this time it's 12pm and he's already done four hours of solid productive, proactive 'move the needle' work. Already twice what the other entrepreneur completed in a whole day, and it's still only lunch time.

He has a healthy lunch and turns off the brain to recover and decompress. It's now 12:45pm, and he's back at his desk, refreshed and raring to go. There are a few pressing issues that take an hour and 15 minutes to resolve before he's able to get back to the work that really matters. It's now 2pm and he gets in another two hours of deep work. Writing sales letters, coming up with new offers, creating new products, forming new strategic partnerships – whatever they might be.

It's now 4pm and time to head home to beat the traffic and see his kids. Again, audiobook on, constantly feeding the brain. Arriving home to play with the kids, bathe them, have dinner. It's now 6:30pm, and he picks up a book written by a proven master in their field on a subject he is looking to improve in his own business. Reading for an hour and a half, again training. It's 8pm before he puts on Netflix or just goofs around with his partner and he's in bed by 9:30pm.

Six hours of deep work. Two hours and 45 minutes of training and sharpening the axe. This adds up to eight hours and 45 minutes of work directed at becoming a master each day – more than three times the other entrepreneur.

Look at how much more training he's able to do and how much more of the work that *really* matters. And it's simply by starting at 4am and being focussed. All this extra ground covered, and this doesn't include the extra day he works on Sundays.

As he keeps working, the years go on and the advantage he has over his competitors just gets wider and wider. Five years down the track and it really doesn't matter how much work the competitor puts in over a given quarter, or if they don't take holidays one year, because they're five years behind. After 10 years, forget about it, it's over. They'll never catch up.

As entrepreneurs, and as people in general, if you want to become truly great at something, there is a choice we have to make. You have to make the inherent sacrifices that come along with it, including hanging out with friends or watching the game on the telly. It's just a matter of what's important to you. If you want to be a master at your craft, you have to make sacrifices.

When you're serious about success, there's no off-season. Nor is there anyone coming to save you. It's just you attacking your goals with gusto and a relentless single parent mother work ethic.

If you follow the principles outlined in this book and do the work, you will be successful – beyond your wildest dreams. I will give you all the tools you need so that you'll never go hungry in life. But like anything worth attaining, it requires a lot of work and dedication.

Are you hungry for it? Willing to put the work in? Fired up?

I thought so!

Let's get busy.

The $500,000 Learning Curve

Before writing this book, I went back and looked at all the money I'd invested in learning what I know today. Seminars I've attended, books I've read, tests I've run, and all the money I've lost along the way…

It added up to **$500,000.**

That's right. Half a million dollars. I could scarcely believe it myself, but it's true. I call this my $500,000 learning curve.

The thing is, looking back I realised that most of that money was spent on useless, ineffective gimmicks peddled by so-called 'gurus' and 'specialists'. People selling the false dream of living on the beach, working an hour a day, and living the high life off a stream of passive income. Or promoting 'secret' tactics to get your website on the front page of Google… only for it to fall off to the 20th page the next day.

None of that stuff worked. None of it.

It was after burning through all that cash I decided to dedicate my time to studying people who had had **real** successes. Masters of advertising, with actual, bankable results across multiple industries, spanning decades of success.

I dedicated myself to studying all the greats from the past 150 years. Guys like Robert Collier, Eugene Schwartz, David Ogilvy, Gary Halbert, and Gary Bencivenga. These guys quietly worked in the background to generate billions of dollars in revenue, often turning tiny businesses into huge household names that are still around today.

If you've never heard of them, Google them! For example, Robert Collier was a 20th-century American author of self-help and New Thought metaphysical books. His book *The Secret of the Ages*, published in 1926, sold over 300,000 copies during his life. Much of what he taught about the art and science of selling are still true today.

I read every book on human psychology I could find. I went deep – like, really deep. What I learned from them completely changed the way I approached business. Some of it worked, some of it didn't. Some of it needed to be completely reimagined to work in today's digital age. And now I'm going to share all of it with you.

I know what you're thinking, why on earth would I share all this knowledge at such a low price point?

It's simple, really. Success doesn't come easy, and it's rare that anyone manages to make their dreams a reality without others opening and holding the door for them from time to time. As you reach for your goals and benefit from the wisdom I'm handing you in this book, don't forget to pass the good sentiment along and help those coming up behind you.

Because if you've done well, it's your obligation to spend

a good portion of your time sending the elevator back down. And that's exactly what I'm doing in this book.

From where am I sending the elevator back down? Well, the strategies and tactics I'm about to walk you through have generated over 1.33 billion– and counting – in revenue for my clients and me.

I've worked with thousands of leaders here in Australia and around the world to help them rapidly and exponentially grow their businesses, by helping them increase that traffic, leads, and sales in the most effective way possible.

In the process, I've learned a thing or two about growing a business fast. This is something, as I've already mentioned, that ultimately comes down to human psychology – the triggers that make people want to buy… or not want to buy.

It's this deep understanding of consumer behaviour and marketing that's turned King Kong into the fastest and most in-demand online marketing agency in Australia, which has been ranked in the top 100 fastest-growing companies in the country two years in a row. We're ranked as the 28th fastest-growing company in the country by The Australian Financial Review. In fact, we're so busy we have a list of clients waiting for their turn to work with us.

Since then I've been called the 'King of Consulting' by Foundr magazine (placed next to Richard Branson, Tony Robbins, and Arianna Huffington!), and have been featured in Forbes, Entrepreneur, Inc Magazine, The Sydney Morning Herald, and hundreds of other notable publications.

Rest assured, I know what I'm talking about. And I'm going to share with you the results of a decade's worth of trial and error, split testing over millions of page views, and millions of dollars in ad spend. You're not going to learn 'the flavour of the month' tactic that's here today but gone tomorrow. You're going to learn strategies that have been successfully deployed for over 150 years!

Long-term strategies you can literally base your business off.

Sadly, today there seems to be an unspoken belief that the most important element behind profitable marketing is simply having the latest software with all the bells and whistles.

The latest landing page builder, CRM software, webinar automation tool, one-page shopping cart checkout system… or a super slick sales funnel.

Go to any marketing forum or Facebook group and you'll see hundreds of questions such as these:

- What's the best landing page builder?

- Which is better WordPress or ClickFunnels?

- How many follow up emails should I have in my funnel?

- Or worse…

- What's the best colour for my call to action button?!

- It's ridiculous but true…

Here is the brutal truth: *None of this matters.*

Why not? Because you can have the most advanced technology, tools, and sales funnel with all the fancy bells, whistles, and advanced marketing automation that delivers a *lame vanilla offer* your prospects simply ignore!

In contrast, this will never beat a white-hot, irresistible offer (developed using 'The Godfather Strategy', which you'll learn about in Phase 4) presented to a starving crowd of your best prospects, presented in a new and unique way – but delivered using simple and rudimentary technology through a basic sales funnel a child could operate.

In the following pages, I will teach you how to do all this and more. These strategies have been tailored to work in today's ruthlessly competitive world of online marketing, and have been proven to work for nearly every business model. Just as importantly, they're easy and straightforward to follow.

First, I'm going to show you how to become the trusted authority in your space against whom all your competitors are measured. Then I'm going to show you how to use that status to have customers practically throwing money at you.

After that, I'll delve into specific strategies and techniques you can use to open the floodgates of traffic, and how to most effectively turn that traffic into customers who buy and buy again.

There are many problems that can occur as a business

grows, but there is only one that's deadly – and that's the inability to bring in new customers in high enough volumes with high enough profit margins.

Once you have systems in place that bring in new, high-paying clients on demand (we'll be covering exactly how to do this in the pages of this book), and once you've got the 'selling' dialled in for your business and you start to scale, you'll eventually let other people take over the one-to-one sales functions. Won't that be amazing? Of course, you'll guide them as the company grows, help them take advantage of opportunities, and work with them to avoid potentially damaging mistakes.

As your business scales and revenues climb, and you have multiple traffic channels bringing in sales, you can let other people do most of the day-to-day selling. However, by establishing your marketing credentials during the first stage, when the selling secrets of your business are still unknown, you'll gain a deep understanding of your business that will serve you well for the rest of your career.

I also personally believe this is a function of the business you should never completely remove yourself from – as we've already established, sales are the lifeblood of your business.

Salesmanship Multiplied: The Most Lethal Skill In Business

Let's go back to the converted shipping container where, as mentioned, I got my start in sales at seventeen.

Remember? I was being yelled at, abused, and I couldn't understand why people were so angry. I asked myself, 'Why won't anybody listen to me?'

It was from pondering this question that I had my first breakthrough. While it might seem obvious, I realised that nobody cared about me, my product, or anything else I was babbling about on the phone.

They cared only about *themselves!* I realised then and there that my pitch had to only be about how I could benefit them. I stopped talking about our company, our products, our services, our mission, or even the name of our company.

If a prospect asked, 'What company are you calling from, I missed that?' I would simply divert back to the reason for my call and switch the focus entirely onto how we could help them. I quickly found the more the call focused on *solving their problem*, the more sales I made.

Once I partnered this with my single parent mother work ethic, I was like a dog on the back of a meat truck. You couldn't shake me once I had this breakthrough.

I was relentless.

I had finally 'cracked the code' and figured out an approach that worked!

The Graduation

After working in this direct sales environment for companies large and small across the world for the better half of a decade, I had a realisation.

I realised no matter how good I got, there were only so many hours in a day. Only so many calls I could make. My income was limited by the clock.

It was at this stage I fell down the rabbit hole of direct response marketing and measured-results marketing. And so, I transitioned from selling one-to-one to selling one-to-many.

I applied my master salesmanship skills to print, audio, video, and other assets I could leverage to multiply those salesmanship skills.

And instead of personally making 300 calls per day, I wrote ads that could call on 300,000 people per day!

It was a quantum shift and a completely different dynamic, an incredibly powerful one where there was no limit to the impact of a sales message.

The ability to write ads and marketing messages that sell is by far the most lethal money-making skill you could ever hope to acquire.

If you master this skill, you should never again have to worry about money.

The ability to write a sales message that brings in

new customers on a profitable basis, consistently and predicably, is the rarest skill on Earth. And, if you can do it – I mean really do it – you can virtually write your own ticket.

The bottom line is, no matter what business you're in and no matter what you're selling, your pursuit for wealth and success will always and forever be served by your ability to craft a *killer sales pitch.*

You can make great money selling one-to-one. But there's a limit. As we know, there are only so many hours in a day, only so many calls you can make, only so many doors you can knock. And, if you limit yourself to one-on-one selling, you'll never really make big money.

To truly make big money, you've got to use an **automated selling system** to get your sales message in front of huge numbers of people all at the same time. 24 hours a day, 7 days a week, 365 days a year.

I look at my sales message as being my salesman soldier. I look at Google Ads, Facebook ads, and radio and YouTube ads as the delivery vehicles I use to deploy that salesman soldier and deliver my message automatically without me having to exert more effort the more times I deliver it.

The reality is that the technology of delivering that sales pitch will be forever changing. Newspapers, direct mail, TV, the Internet, Google, Facebook, LinkedIn, YouTube, Twitter, Snapchat... The list will go on into perpetuity.

The way you deliver your sales message may change

abruptly and radically. Yet what you put into that message will always be based on the classic tools of world-class salesmanship and human psychology.

Listen carefully: You can always hire people to deliver the work, set up the technology, do your company accounts and tax returns.

But the guys who know how to craft a killer sales pitch that forces people to whip out their wallet and throw money at you will always be rare... incredibly valued... outrageously well paid... and sitting in the driver's seat of their abundant future.

Good advertising is simply a sales pitch. Or better put, salesmanship multiplied.

Your advertisement and sales message should act like an army of tiny salesmen soldiers. And they should go forth, regardless of the delivery medium, and deliver a concert pitch.

If you're running a YouTube ad that's viewed by 200,000 people, that's 200,000 chances to give your best sales pitch. It's 200,000 separate prospects all seeing and hearing your ad via one-on-one communication.

Think about it this way – if you had a chance to make a 60-second sales pitch 80,000 times to 80,000 prospects, what would you say to them during those 60 seconds to give the most compelling information, build the most desire, make the best case, and reduce the risk for them to take the next step?

What would you say? If you were right there in person, in front of your dream buyer? Would you blurt out, 'Here's our stuff — come buy from us for no justifiable or rational reason'?

I hope not! Sadly, most advertising you see and hear is weak and vague. It would be taken hostage and eaten alive by the money-multiplying soldiers described above.

You see, after coming into contact with tens of thousands of business owners every month and speaking with thousands from all over the world, I've noticed that not even 1% of businesses put together advertising that builds any kind of a case for a prospect to want to buy their products or services. Instead, it just fires features and benefits at the prospect, serving no more purpose than to announce, 'We exist, so buy our stuff', instead of giving a compelling reason why they should do business with you.

A good example of this sort of 'here's-my-stuff-come-buy-from-us' advertising can be found on any Google search results page.

Just do a search on 'financial planners'. Here's what most say: 'Financial Planning Services, Friendly & Trusted Experts, Tailor-Made Advice, Trusted Advisors, 30+ Years of Experience, blah blah blah....'

Every single ad basically says the same thing. It's impossible for a prospect to make an intelligent decision about whom to call based on any criteria other than who's got the prettiest website.

The prospect can't determine if any of the products or

services are any better or any worse or different than those offered by the sea of competitors.

This situation is true for any medium. Your ads should make a red-hot pitch for your product or service in the same way as a salesperson would in a face-to-face selling situation.

Look at your ads. If you were talking live to a hot prospect, your dream buyer, would you say the same thing your current advertising says to convince them to buy from you? If you'd say something different, then you need to light those ads on fire and rethink your whole advertising strategy.

When somebody is considering buying something, the one thing they want is information — useful, helpful, no-nonsense information. The more information you can give them in your ads, the better your chance to generate an action.

Before we get deeper into the quality of your information, let's first talk about a problem that vexes many business owners: the level of traffic to their website or store.

The Biggest Misconception

When it comes to growing sales, businesses generally have one or more of the following challenges to overcome:

SMALL LIST: Your list may be small or even non-existent. Meaning, you don't have a large enough database of prospects or previous clients you can call upon to generate tens of thousands of dollars on demand.

LOW TRAFFIC: Meaning you're simply not getting enough people to your website, store, or landing page.

LOW CONVERSIONS: If you're getting enough traffic but you aren't seeing as many leads and sales as you want, then you have a conversion problem. Meaning, what you're offering simply isn't compelling your prospects to buy.

People often ask me, 'Sabri, I really want to grow my business and I just need more traffic... Can I hire you to get me more traffic?' Most of the time they're looking for the latest 'hack' to triple their traffic... A golden Google leprechaun that skyrockets their rankings... The latest Facebook ad tactics to increase their click-through rate... Or the Instagram bot that secretly follows people and reaches into their pockets and deposits their money into the company's bank account.

But you don't need the latest traffic hack. You see, in today's day and age, traffic is a commodity. Just like milk, bread, or a pack of Tim Tams. If you want to buy groceries, you go to a supermarket. And if you want to buy traffic, you go to a traffic supermarket.

Just like a supermarket where you can go and buy as many groceries as you want or can afford, you can also go to a traffic supermarket and buy as many website visitors as you want or need. Literally, as many as you can handle! Never have businesses had such instant access to millions of consumers within minutes. Now, when it comes to traffic, there are only two names worth mentioning. You can think of them as the Woolworths and Coles of the online traffic world. They are Google and Facebook. And they account for more than 90% of traffic online.

Get this: On Google, people make 3.5 billion searches per day. As for Facebook, there are over 16 million active users in Australia alone. You can have a Google Ads account set up and running in under 30 minutes, giving you access to literally millions or billions of people within hours. Or you could set up a Facebook Ad campaign in a couple of hours and have access to the 1.8 million Aussies who log on every day!

We're living in an age where you have access to millions of prospects within hours. It's incredible, and I could go on about this for hours, but here's my point: If there is so much traffic available at your fingertips, and you can literally go and buy as much as you want at any time, then why do businesses say they have a traffic problem?

The truth is this: *They don't have a traffic problem!*

They have a conversion problem. When you really think about it, this traffic complaint makes zero sense. How can you have a traffic problem when digital marketing has made traffic more abundant then it's ever been? The real issue here is not in buying traffic. Anyone with an internet connection and a credit card can do that.

The real issue is converting that traffic into actual sales using a system based on unit economics that makes

buying traffic profitable and self-liquidating. Meaning it pays for itself like a modern-day golden goose. I've spent millions of dollars battle-testing different traffic sources and marketing strategies for our clients. After all this testing, I came to one conclusion:

If you want to land those high-value clients like clockwork and grow your business to $1,000,000 a month in revenue or beyond without spending 70 or 80 hours a week in your business, then you need an **automated lead generation and client conversion system** that turns advertising into profit.

You need a system you can put $1 in which generates $2, $5, $10, $50 or even $200 back. You see, the most dependable and predictable way to grow sales and generate wealth is to turn *advertising into profit.*

And if you can't pay money to acquire a new customer, then you don't have a business. Let me say that again: If you can't pay money to acquire a new customer, you do not have a business.

If you're solely relying on free traffic, referrals, joint ventures, or other channels like these, then you don't have a predictable and dependable way to grow your business. You're simply at the whim of whatever fate drops in your lap. However, generating a return on investment from paid advertising is like pulling a lever and having cash drop into your account. It's *predictable, repeatable, and scalable.*

This isn't something I made up because I thought it was cute. We've helped small businesses flourish into multi-million-dollar companies using this approach. And it's grounded in the same principles used by some of the world's wealthiest investors.

A Wiser Investment Than Savings, Stocks, Or Real Estate

Instead of relying on luck to deliver you customers and cash injections when you need them, you must do what billionaires do. Invest in assets and get returns on those assets. Look at how much return some of the most prolific billionaire investors in the world are getting from their assets:

Carl Icahn: 31% annual returns

Warren Buffett: 20% annual returns

George Soros: 20% annual returns

Peter Lynch: 29% annual returns

Clearly, these giants of investing are not relying on referrals to average a 20% annual rate of return or more. They are putting in $1 and getting $1.20 or $1.30 back on a predictable, billion-dollar scale.

In other words, they maximise and leverage money to make more money.

And think about this...

These are the most famous and wealthy investors in

history and they're completely happy to invest billions to generate a return of just 20-30% per year. More on why this is important in just a moment.

First, let me ask you this: What are some of the ways you could try and leverage your money? And what kind of returns could you get?

Remember – you're not a billionaire or genius investor, so you're going to have rely on something simpler and more accessible to get the same results.

Let's look at some options together, starting with high-interest saving accounts or term deposits. If you were to invest in a high-interest savings account, you'd typically look at a 2-3% annual return. In other words, you put $1 in and get $1.03. This isn't great, right?

	Initial Deposit $ 50000	Monthly Deposit $ 1000	Period 12 months					Calculate
Compare		Maximum Variable Rate p.a.	Standard Variable Rate p.a.	Bonus Interest p.a.	Fees	Min Bal / Min Deposit	Interest Earned	
ME Online Savings Account	Ongoing, variable 3.05% p.a. rate when you link to a ME Everyday Transaction account and make a weekly purchase with your Debit MasterCard using tap & go. Available on balances up to $250,000.	3.05%	1.30%	1.75%	$0	$0 / $0	$1,715.68	Open More
Citibank Online Saver	Introductory rate of 3.00% p.a. for 4 months, reverting to a rate of 1.70% p.a. Available on balances below $500,000.	3.00%	1.70%	1.30%	$0	$0 / $0	$1,177.61	Open More
ING DIRECT Savings Maximiser	Ongoing, variable 3.00% p.a. when you link to an ING Orange Everyday bank account and deposit $1,000+ each month. Available on balances up to $100,000.	3.00%	1.60%	1.40%	$0	$0 / $0	$1,687.18	Open More
RaboDirect High Interest Savings Account	Introductory rate of 3.05% p.a. for 4 months, reverting to a rate of 2.00% p.a. Available on balances below $250,000	3.05%	2.00%	1.05%	$0	$0 / $0	$1,303.64	Open More
Bankwest Hero Saver	Ongoing, variable 2.65% p.a. rate when you deposit at least $200 each month and make no withdrawals. Available on balances up to $250,000.	2.65%	0.01%	2.64%	$0	$0 / $0	$1,488.04	Open More
AMP Saver Account	Introductory rate of 2.55% p.a. for 4 months, reverting to a rate of 2.10% p.a. Available on balances below $5,000,000.	2.55%	2.10%	0.45%	$0	$0 / $0	$1,255.13	Open More

So, what about stocks and bonds? A recent report by the Australian Stock Exchange showed that over the last 30 years, Australian shares have produced a 9.5% return per annum on investments. In other words, you put $1 in and get $1.09 after a year.

Australian and global shares
$10,000 growth over the past 30 years to 30 June 2016
Logarithmic scale

But these are just two examples, so let's look at another. There are a lot of people making a ton of money from real estate and property investment, right?

Well, real estate investment has yielded an average annual return of 11.8% per year over the last 20 years. Now that's better than the others – on average – but it's still not the kind of money that could transform your life and build wealth fast. You're still only getting 11 cents for every dollar you put in.

Not very inspiring. But you'll be happy to find out that **investing in your business, more specifically your advertising, smashes these woeful returns on investment.**

Look at this advertising expenditure from one of my client's Facebook accounts. $4,403.64 was spent for a return of $17,850.00. That's $13,446 in profit in just two days. That's a return on investment of 305%!

Even if you consider product costs of 30-40%, this business is still making an unbelievable return from its advertising investment. They put in $1 and got $4.05 back. Or more specifically in their case... put in $4,403.64 and got $17,850.00 back!

Here's another example from Facebook. The advertising spend is $7,334.06 and the return is $104,683.48! That's a 1,356.96% ROI! In other words, they put in $1 and got $14.27 back. Or once again, specifically, they put $7,334.06 in and got $104,683.48 back! If that doesn't get you excited, I'm not sure what to say.

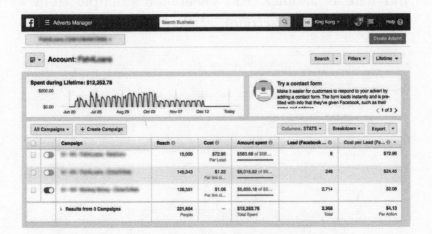

But here's another example. In this case, we were generating leads for a business. We spent $12,252.75 and generated 2,968 leads! The cost was just $4.13 per lead.

And for this client a lead wasn't just a name, email, and phone number. It was a 16-step application asking all types of information, resulting in super qualified buyers. In fact, because they were targeting high-value prospects, they only needed one or two of the leads to become clients to make back that $12k investment. And they got 2,968 leads.

And here is another lead generation example from a client's Google Ads account:

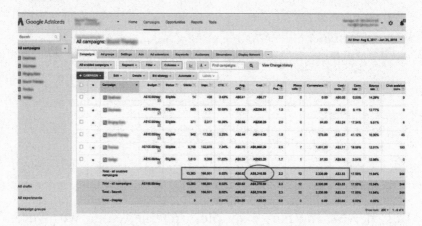

We spent $8,310.59 and generated 2,330 leads at just $3.53 per lead. This was for a client selling a product retailing for $1,000. Again, this is insane ROI!

Here's another example of one of my client's Google Ads account:

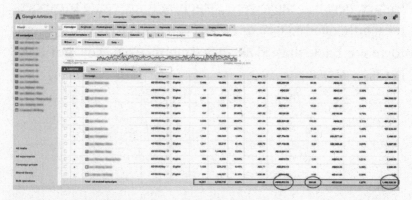

Over four months we spent $46,792.25 on AdWords to generate $1,490,028.30! That's a 3,084% ROI! They put in $1 and got $31.84 back.

One last example. Here's another client for whom we generated a huge ROI. Over four months we spent $8,132 on Facebook to generate $34,579. That's a 325% ROI!

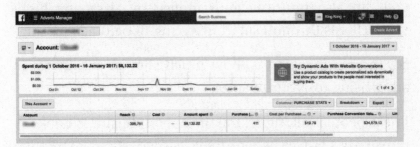

Anyway, I think you get the point. Investing in advertising that attracts high-value prospects and then converts that traffic into bona fide sales and clients is the smartest, most lucrative investment you'll ever make.

And those were just examples of Facebook Ads. That's not taking into account SEO, Google Ads, remarketing, or any of the other traffic channels we employ for our clients to multiply money.

Yet despite this reliable, lucrative return, many businesses brag that they don't spend money on advertising. They almost wear it as a 'badge of honour'. And usually they don't advertise because they think of it as an expense. However, that's a huge tell-tale sign that you're playing too small. You see…

Advertising is an investment that makes more money than anything else. Period.

But it's not your typical investment, where you stick a bunch of money into something and hope you end up rich when you're old. Because when done properly, advertising can make you money almost immediately. Just like billionaires who leverage money to make more money, you can also multiply your money by attracting high-value clients through smart investing in paid advertising.

So, the big question is, how much should you invest in advertising for your business?

I hear people talking all the time about business books or university courses where they learned about marketing budgets and having a 'defined budget' as a percentage of sales.

Like you should spend 10% of turnover on marketing, and ridiculous things of that nature. Let me tell you: You should only have a marketing budget if your marketing isn't working. Because if you're putting $1 in and getting $3 back... Why wouldn't you want to invest as much as your cash flow allows? In some cases, it may even make sense to borrow cash to invest in marketing, as you have essentially created a money-printing machine.

The way I think about it, it's like a vending machine that you can put in a dollar and buy a $5 or a $10 note. Essentially, you're buying money at a steep discount! And why would you limit yourself to how much you should spend? I don't know an investment on the planet that gives the types of returns that efficient paid advertising does, except perhaps super high-risk, start-up unicorns. Warren Buffett himself, the most successful investor in the world, only gets a 20% return.

In the pages that follow I'll be revealing to you my secret selling system and how I achieved staggering results for thousands of businesses of all types.

I've systematised this process and am handing it to you on a silver platter. Over a decade of trial and error, millions of dollars spent on scientific advertising tests, measured down to the dollar – you'll find all this and more in the following chapter.

Buckle up, take notes, and enjoy!

PHASE 1:

Understand And Identify Your Dream Buyer

Most online marketing information you've learned is dead wrong. I know that's a big call to make – but it's true.

The fact is, no matter how much you've been taught about digital marketing in the past, you haven't been told the full story.

None of the common digital marketing strategies and tactics you've been taught will ever give you the rapid growth you seek without first understanding the principles you're going to learn in this book.

It's true: the indispensable strategies for success have been kept secret from you. This is the vital knowledge the 'gurus' don't tell you and don't want you to know.

Why would they keep these hidden from you? The answer is simple.

Most 'gurus' *simply don't know them.* Or are too lazy to implement them.

They're not easy to sell to business owners and entrepreneurs.

You see, contrary to what you've been told, it's not simply all about traffic and getting thousands of visitors to your site.

Nor is it all about the latest sales funnel software or Google hack that will open the floodgate to free traffic.

The reality is that competition online is at an all-time

high. With the rising cost per click in Google Ads, or the competition with SEO and Facebook ads, the online marketplace is so fiercely competitive that you must have a solid strategy to convert traffic into actual leads, customers, and revenue.

If you don't, you'll end up wasting your money and your competitors will eat you alive.

The mainstream way of 'solving' this problem is to target only the people most likely to buy your products and services. I'm going to show you why this approach is so misguided.

The Larger Market Formula

One of the secrets to skyrocketing sales is by appealing to a larger market. The Larger Market Formula breaks down the entire audience of buyers in any market into four key categories:

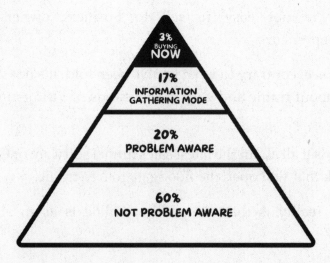

Let's start at the top of the pyramid.

In any given market at any given time, 3% of people are in 'buying mode'. If you pick up the newspaper, watch TV, or do a Google search, you'll see ads shouting, 'We have the biggest range and the best prices!' These ads are directed at that 3%, and the conversation goes something like this:

'I'm thirsty right now'.

'Would you like this crisp glass of fresh water?'

'Yes please!'

That's not hard. A high percentage of the 3% will buy. You might get a few objections like, 'I don't want room temperature water. Can you give it to me chilled?' Not hard to rectify.

The problem is, your competitors are going hard after that top 3%. If you split up that 3% of easy customers between you and your competitors, you're never going to make much money.

The real money is in the 37% of people who are saying, 'I'm kinda thirsty – what should I drink?' They are either gathering information (17%) or 'problem aware' (20%).

Or how about those who don't even know they're thirsty to begin with – because this market is a whopping 60% of all people! Once you understand the Larger Market Formula, you can use it to swoop up the majority of the market that's being ignored – and transform them into loyal customers who continually drive sales into your business.

The goal is to move the 97% of potential customers up the pyramid faster. Because believe it or not, even 'disinterested' prospects can turn into lucrative customers if you know how to approach them. The problem is that most people treat every lead like the 3% who are ready to buy now. They have no systems in place to capture and nurture the other 97%.

How To Take Customers From 'Just Looking' To 'Shut Up And Take My Money'

To reach the 97% who aren't ready to buy now (but could be very soon), you have to educate them. When a prospect isn't informed or knowledgeable on a subject, they're in a state of uncertainty and people don't buy in this state. But the more they know, the more likely they are to buy.

The bonus here is, if *you* are the one educating them, you're also making sure that when they hit the 'buy now' stage, they'll be likely to buy from *you*. To do this, your message must be powerful, insightful, and education-based, and not simply a promotional piece about your company.

What's also happening is that you're changing the dynamics and psychology of the relationship between your business and your potential customers. It's a technique that means you're no longer chasing clients. Instead, they're putting their hands up and requesting to speak to you.

They want you to help them. They start pursuing you or calling you to enquire about your products and services. It's a game changer, and it's hands down the best way to attract business online.

We go deeper into this later in the book, but...

The key is to install a system that:

- Attracts

- Educates

- Nurtures

- Gets prospects to act!

This is vitally important for any business looking to grow rapidly and consistently. Because when you have a system that takes cold traffic from Google, Facebook, or any other channel and 'warms it up', you're only talking to interested prospects, not time-wasters.

You're no longer spending hours trying to educate a customer that your solution is the best; you're just closing and collecting the cash.

Your *systems* – not you – are doing the grunt work in educating prospects, following them up, and delivering content that educates. And when they reach out to you, you'll know they are predisposed, pre-qualified, ready, willing, and able to do business with you. They're virtually 99% ready to buy.

Here's what you need to do:

- Educate your prospects so they know more about the process of solving their problem, and they're empowered to make a better buying decision. (Do this using a High-Value Content Offer, i.e. free reports, videos, cheat sheets, or other value-based materials. You'll learn how to do this in Phase 2.)

- Take your best sales pitch or frequently asked questions and turn them into assets that nurture prospects on autopilot. At the same time as giving them information, you're also moving them up the pyramid. (Do this using the Magic Lantern Technique, which you'll learn in Phase 6.)

- Position your solution as the obvious choice.

- Make them an irresistible offer using 'The Godfather Strategy'. (You'll learn how to do this in Phase 4.)

If you can actively and skilfully move people up the pyramid, you can shift many of the 97% of prospects from 'not buying right now' or 'not even thinking about it' to becoming your customer right away.

The best part about this is you get to reach your dream customers before they even know they're ready to buy, thus reaching them well before your competitors have the chance.

The best way to do this is through what's called a sales *funnel.* This technique shifts a prospect up each stage of the pyramid over a period of a few weeks. Done right, you'll easily see your sales double without having to spend more on your advertising.

We'll go into sales funnels in Phase 5, but in simple terms, a sales funnel is a controlled path an online user takes to become a website visitor, then a prospect, and finally a customer. It's a way to convert prospects from uninterested, confused wanderers into your best customers.

The Halo Strategy: Know Your Customer!

Before you start thinking about a sales funnel, creating offers, or setting up Google Ads, Facebook Ads, SEO, or any other system, you need to do this one thing, as nothing matters if you can't nail this:

You must know your customer intimately!

When it comes to acquiring new customers, the most basic starting point is understanding who they are. When you understand this, you can tailor your marketing message directly for your audience.

Many businesses fall into the trap of believing they know who their customers are. They acquire rudimentary data such as their gender, age, and perhaps even their location, and stop right there. This is a big mistake, because knowing them intimately can make the difference between winning and losing.

Here are two important points:

- Understanding someone's age and gender is not enough to really know them.

- "Anyway, your competition is already doing this, so with this minimalist approach, the best you can do is match their data".

For your message to stand out from the crowd and really win customers, **you must go deeper. Much deeper.**

You need to uncover your customer's deepest and most primal desires. You must delve into their fears, hopes, wishes, and dreams. This is the stuff they're thinking but don't tell anyone. You need to move beyond the obvious and work out how your audience thinks, feels, and acts. As Robert Collier said…

"Enter the conversation already taking place in the customer's mind".

So how do you *really* identify your 'dream buyer'?

Your dream buyer can be identified through Pareto's principle of the 80/20 rule.

How?

Because the Pareto Principle is *exponential!*

Let me explain. We already know that 20% of your customers represent 80% of your revenue. But within that initial 20%, the 80/20 rule also applies.

Meaning the top 20% of the top 20% of your customers (or the top 4% overall) represent 64% of your sales (calculated as 80% times 80%).

Meaning you can laser in on the 4% of your customers who contribute to 64% of your business's revenues, and importantly, find more customers like them.

Your Power 4%

I call these customers your Power 4%. Why? Because they have the power to make you filthy rich!

Once you identify your Power 4%, you want to learn all about them. Not just the usual stuff like age, gender, location, what products or services they enquired about, and how they found you or what channel they came in from (although you want to know that too). You need to know them much more intimately.

You need to read your prospect's mind. You must be obsessed with their passions, dreams, fears, and desires. Getting to know all this crucial detail is what we call **The Halo Strategy.** It's the most powerful strategy of them all and the most important to get right – as none of the other stuff matters if you can't nail this.

Once you identify your Power 4%, you want to look at what characteristics they share. Start with the obvious data including age, location, and education level. In addition to this, you then need to look at what products or services they enquired about and how they found you or what channel they came in from. This gives you incredibly valuable information you can use with a variety of marketing tools to find *the same type of customers* out there who don't know about your business yet.

So where do you start to discover your market's hopes and dreams, pains and fears, those that literally keep them up at night tossing and turning and unable to sleep? It's simple. All you need to get started is two or three major keywords or search phrases around your products or services. Once you have those in place, it's time to do some detective work. You can download the halo strategy worksheet at - https://resources.selllikecrazy.co/

HALO
STRATEGY

Theme	Most Common	2nd Most Frequent	3rd Most Frequent	Score of Importance (1/10)
Hopes & Dreams				3
				7
				10
				2
Pains & Fears				
Barriers & Uncertainties				

Glossary of Verbiage, Jargon and Niche-Specific Terms or Language	
Term	Description

Think about the one or two major keywords and search terms people use to search for your products or services.

- Search on Google for popular blogs, LinkedIn forums, YouTube comment sections, Amazon reviews, Reddit, Quora, and social media platforms. Go wherever your audience hangs out and congregates.

- Look at what your audience is saying and feeling. What are they happy with? What are they unhappy with? Look at their concerns and questions. Notice any themes? Are they banging their head against the wall on the same issue over and over? Pay close attention to the language they're using when it comes to the existing products and services already on the market.

- Once you've collected all your information, organise your findings into categories of comments or concerns that appear the most, noting what feelings were most dominant.

Find the gaps or shortcomings in the products or services already out there. This gap is your winning ticket and a way for you to tap into the hearts and minds of your audience.

We'll be using all this research in the next Phase to attract your dream buyer.

To read the mind of your prospects and know exactly the questions they're asking during the research and buying cycle, the auto-suggest results provided by Google and Bing are a goldmine of insights.

As you type into the search bar, you're presented with an aggregated view of the questions and therefore a hint of the motivations and emotions of the people behind each search query. It's perhaps one of the best but most underutilised sources of research for content ideas.

Answerthepublic.com

The next best thing to actually reading your customer's mind is AnswerThePublic.com. This tool is one of the best-kept secrets in the sales and marketing industry, and it will give you invaluable insight into what your customers are thinking.

At AnswerThePublic, you type in your keyword or search phrase and the tool generates a diagram of related searches. Depending on your search term, you can get hundreds of results that give you direct insight into what your audience is thinking, the kind of questions they're asking, and the hot-button issues they're struggling with. And once you know their questions and issues, you can provide the solution.

At the time of writing this, the tool is free, but I'm sure they will be coming up with a paid model shortly.

It's an absolute goldmine of data for the modern-day marketer and perhaps one of the best but most underutilised sources of research for the questions that plague today's markets. Read on to learn how to get the best out of this tool.

Let's use 'homebuilder' as an example. If we start to search for 'homebuilder', this tool spits out all the questions people are having related to this query:

'HomeBuilder' Questions 42 Visualisation Data

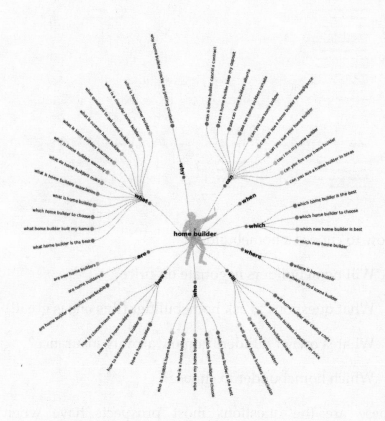

How to choose a homebuilder

- Will homebuilders negotiate on price?

- What questions to ask homebuilder (this one is great!)

- What is owner builders home warranty insurance?

- Which homebuilder to choose?

These are the questions most prospects have when thinking about engaging a homebuilder. We'll be using these hair-on-fire questions in the next step to attract our dream buyer, and you will do the same in your market so you know you're solving real problems of real people looking for your products or services.

Other great places to look are Facebook Groups and pages around your market and niche. These are goldmines for valuable information.

These are what you want to look through:

- All posts by the page owner

- All posts by visitors to a fan page

- Count of engagements for a post by page owner

- Count of engagements by post type

You don't need to scroll through pages and pages of comments. You can simply look at the most popular ones and read what the market is discussing and thinking about.

Another incredible source for market intel is to look at threads on Reddit and question platform website, Quora. These are like walking into a golden palace of customer insight and eavesdropping on thousands of conversations that are taking place behind closed doors about your market.

After you've used the Halo Strategy, it's now time to use the marketing intel and research you've gathered to create your dream buyer avatar.

Creating Your Dream Buyer Avatar

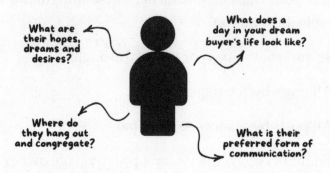

What are their hopes, dreams and desires?

What does a day in your dream buyer's life look like?

Where do they hang out and congregate?

What is their preferred form of communication?

Knowing your dream buyer changes everything – your product and service offering, your marketing strategy, value proposition, pricing, tone of your copy, what channels you advertise on, and more.

No one can afford to address everyone's problems, especially in today's market conditions where the media we use to reach our customers is so highly fragmented. If your business is going to compete with the big guys, you have to zero in on your dream buyer.

A lot of business owners simply say, 'I'm targeting whoever is interested in my services'. Some say that their target is business owners, homeowners, property investors, or mothers. It's a good start, but these targets are much too general to go after. Specificity is key.

And while defining your dream buyer might seem like you are excluding other audiences who might buy from you, keep in mind that targeting a specific dream buyer doesn't mean you have to exclude anyone who doesn't fit that criteria.

The purpose of going after a dream buyer is to focus your message and marketing budget on whichever market is most likely to buy your products, as well as those prospects who would be your dream customers.

Focusing on your dream buyer brings clarity to your marketing message, and your copy becomes sharp and hard like the tip of a spear that cuts through the noise in your marketplace, which ultimately leads to a more profitable business.

And look, while you might be thinking that creating a dream buyer persona isn't the sexiest thing, let me tell you this:

Advertising channels change. Landing page builder software changes. Algorithms change. Tactics change. But the fundamentals of learning what people want, understanding exactly where you can help them, and then telling the right people about it in the most persuasive way are timeless strategies that worked 100 years ago and will work 1,000 years from now.

This chapter is about getting to know the right people – your dream buyers – who will benefit the most and pay you most for your products and services.

Here are the nine essential questions to ask in the process of defining your ideal customer. Let's get started.

Nine Questions To Define Your Dream Buyer

1. Where does your dream buyer hang out and congregate?

Name both online and offline places where your dream buyers hang out and congregate. The more detailed and specific, the better.

'Hangs out on Facebook' is too general.

'Hangs out in the Mothers of Melbourne Facebook group' is more precise and actionable.

'Likes the outdoors' is too general to mean anything insightful and actionable.

'Likes going to the park every Saturday morning with her two kids' shows habits and values and is specific.

'Reads blogs' isn't targeted enough.

'Obsessively reads Rockin Mama, Mamavation, and Reddit' is defined and revealing.

Knowing exactly where your dream buyers are hanging out influences a lot of things including where you should advertise, what you should advertise, the tone of your copy, and vernacular to use.

2. Where does your dream buyer get their information?

When your dream buyer is in research mode, where do

they go to find the answers they seek? Is it Google? A particular blog? Books? Magazines? YouTube?

Write your findings as a simple sentence: 'When Sally is curious about a topic, the first place she goes is Google search on her iPhone'.

3. What are their biggest frustrations and challenges?

Truly understanding and empathising with their biggest frustrations and challenges are the most important keys to defining your dream buyer avatar.

By knowing what it's like walking in your customer's shoes, you'll be able to create better products and services that address their specific pain points and problems.

Here are a few examples to get your creative juices flowing:

'I wish someone would just write this sales copy for me'.

'I need to lose ten kilos before my wedding'.

'Ugh. I wish I could just have someone run my Facebook ads for me'.

Your dream buyer's frustrations and challenges are integral to the products and services you offer. Whatever it is you are selling has to solve a problem large enough that your dream buyer will happily part with their hard-earned money for you to solve it for them.

Knowing their biggest frustration and challenges also will determine the emotions you speak to in your copy and advertising. There are a number of emotions behind the challenges and frustrations your dream buyer is experiencing – they could be sadness, anger, fear, remorse, hope, a desire for something better. By speaking to exactly what your dream buyer is feeling, you'll be able to connect with them emotionally on more than just a rational level.

It will also reflect the types of stories you tell. The logic here is simple. When your dream buyer sees a testimonial from a customer who solved their biggest frustrations and challenges with your product or service, then they are more likely to buy from you. They can see this positive transformation take place in someone else.

4. What are their hopes, dreams, and desires?

Knowing your dream buyer's hopes, dreams and desires helps you paint a vivid picture of what life could be like after using your products and services. Think of it as selling the dream and painting a picture of the Promised Land.

When your products or services help your dream buyer attain their hopes, dreams, and desires, it becomes much easier to write copy for your landing pages, website, ads, and other assets you leverage to sell more goods and services.

Here are a few examples of copy written to speak to a dream buyer's desires:

CUSTOMER DESIRE COPY	COPY SPEAKING TO THEIR DESIRES
• *'I want to lose 10kgs before my wedding day'*	• *'Our exercise program is specifically designed to help you get shredded FAST and drop 10kgs-15kgs in 60 days guaranteed!'*
• *'I want to have my website ranked higher on Google'*	• *'Guaranteed Google rankings in 90 days or we work for free!'*
• *'I'm worried someone will break into my house and steal all my possessions that I've worked so hard to get'*	• *'Our 24/7 security service makes your home almost impenetrable by crooks, thieves and robbers. Keeping your belongings and family safe'*

5. What are their biggest fears?

What are your dream buyer's deepest fears? What keeps them up at night, tossing and turning, unable to sleep? What do they worry about in their mind but never tell anyone? Fully understanding your market's deepest and most primal fears is an often overlooked component to crafting a customer avatar. However, in my opinion, it's equally as important, if not more, than understanding their hopes, dreams, and desires. Why? People are motivated more by pain than they are by pleasure. They are more motivated by fear of loss than they are by the desire to gain something. Therefore, calling out their fears in your copy and ads is an incredibly important element to get your dream buyer to take action and motivate them to move away from what they fear most.

A good example of fear used to motivate people into taking action is the approach used by insurance companies. They call out their prospects' deepest fears more than they do the benefits of getting covered.

Example:

'Life insurance can help ease your worries that your loved ones will be taken care of and may not have to deal with the financial strain that could arise from you no longer being around, or the financial hardship that can impact your kids through their surviving parent. If you have a partner, would he or she be able to take care of the kids without your help? Prevent your partner's financial hardship affecting your kids' welfare and future'.

6. What is their preferred form of communication?

Email? Text? Chat? Facebook Live? Or do they prefer physical mail? This is a matter of where your audience wants you to communicate with them. The fundamental lesson here is to communicate with your customers where they already are. Don't try and move them onto something that is more convenient for you rather than where they already are.

7. What phrases, exact language, and vernacular do they use?

As previously mentioned, Robert Collier has this fantastic

quote: 'Enter the conversation already taking place in the customer's mind'.

You see, there is already language and niche-specific terms being used in your customer's mind for their hopes, dreams, pain, fears, and desires. Your job is to listen and write them down. What industry terminology are they using, what specific vernacular and niche-specific terms?

When using The Halo Strategy to conduct research on where your buyers are hanging out and congregating, you must document the exact phrases and terminology they use and store them in a spreadsheet to spark ideas for website copy, landing pages, and ads. Take specific comments from Reddit, Facebook Group, or YouTube, and document your audience's word-for-word responses.

In today's day and age, scepticism is rampant. Now more than ever, people are attracted to people (and businesses) who speak their language, get their sense of humour, or share the same point of view. Every time they read your copy, your goal is for your dream buyer to say to themselves, 'Whoa, it's like they're talking directly to me'.

8. What does a day in your dream buyer's life look like?

7:05am - Mike wakes up to the sound of marimbas on his iPhone's alarm clock.

7:15am – Checks his inbox to make sure the world isn't coming to an end from any emails that came in overnight. Then opens up Instagram to see who's commenting and liking his latest post.

8:10am - Brews the new Colombian roast using his shiny new French press.

8:32am - Stuck in traffic on Punt road listening to his favourite Drake playlist on Spotify.

9:03am - Gets into the office.

9:18am - Checks email and calendar.

10:01am – Checks the stats in Google Analytics, Facebook Ads, and custom dashboard.

10:40am – Has a meeting with his team about current week.

12:05pm - Eats favourite Poké bowl from new hipster joint on the corner.

1:12pm – On his way back to the office, checks Instagram, Facebook, and LinkedIn.

2:04pm - Afternoon lull, wishing his office had a nap pod for him to have a siesta.

2:38pm – Write new Facebook Ads and email sequence.

4:05pm - Brainstorms how to generate more leads to meet quarterly growth goals and revenue targets.

6:15pm - Drives home ready for a House of Cards marathon on Netflix.

Imagining what your ideal customer's daily life looks like adds an incredible personal element to your marketing. It also becomes practical – when is the best time to email your prospects? When are they most likely to respond? When are they most attentive?

Your dream buyer is a completely different person at 8am on a Monday morning than at 6:30pm on a Friday. Be aware of this and use it in your marketing.

9. What makes them happy?

The customer journey is more than the exchange of money for goods and services. Your clients are emotional beings, and people want to interact with companies and brands that make them feel good about themselves.

Where are the touch points in your dream buyer's journey where you can insert surprises, do the unexpected, be remarkable, and bring a smile to their face? Maybe it's a handwritten thank-you note after signing up for your service, a personalised email sent on their birthday, or a free box full of company swag and cookies (who doesn't love cookies?).

Inserting happiness into the buyer's journey can create a deeper level of emotional connection that cultivates loyal and raving fans for the long term.

The End Result

After answering all of these questions, write a paragraph summarising your findings. It could look like this summary of Sally, the dream buyer for a new app focused on environmentally-friendly mothers:

'Sally loves spending time reading stories and getting

tips from other mums, and learning about parenthood in the Mothers of Melbourne Facebook group. It's a much cherished pastime of hers. Her biggest frustration being a mother of two is simply that there is not enough hours in the day to do everything. When she's in research mode, the first place she goes is Google on her iPad in the kitchen. She's a frequent (kinda obsessive) visitor of mummy blogs like Rockin Mama and Mamavation. Her life-long dream is to start her own interior design business, so she can have a creative outlet and more 'me time'. Last week when she was shopping at her local farmers market and browsing Instagram, an ad popped up with an invitation to download a new app for environmentally-friendly cleaning products'.

The end result is a much deeper, more intimate understanding of where and how to reach your dream buyers, and how to speak to them. The compounding result will cause massive breakthroughs that geometrically grow your business and allow you to dominate your market.

Defining your target market is one of the hardest parts of starting a business. The good news is that once you do it, everything else will quickly start falling into place. You just have to figure out which medium to use to effectively reach them, and which marketing strategies they respond to.

Action Points

- Identify the 20% of customers who account for 80% of your sales volume and profits, and your Power 4% of customers.

- Using The Halo Strategy, identify what they struggle with.

- Organise your findings.

- Create your dream buyer customer.

PHASE 2:

Create The Perfect Bait For Your Dream Buyer

I'm about to describe the most unsuspecting way to outsell the most ferocious competition in your marketplace, even when their marketing is brilliant, their budget is huge, and their products and services are half the price of yours.

I'm going to show you how to create a High-Value Content Offer that sucks in leads like a vacuum cleaner on steroids!

With the insights gained in Phase 1, your next move is to create the most irresistible bait for your dream buyer. In this chapter, I will help you identify the prospects who are interested in what you're selling but who want more information, which you're going to give to them. This way, they'll have more of what they need to make an informed decision and move up the pyramid from the research phase to the buying phase.

This allows you to generate hundreds of leads while positioning yourself as a trusted authority almost instantly – even if nobody's heard of you!

As an example, we'll take a homebuilding company because it's easy to see how a small shift has huge benefits.

The typical full-page new home ad has the company name at the top and some sort of 'SALE' or 'DISPLAY HOMES NOW OPEN' headline predominantly placed.

It's exactly the same as all the other homebuilders taking up all the other advertisement pages. They're practically leaving it to random chance to compete for their share of that 3% of people who are buying now. Now imagine the ad began with this headline:

WARNING: Do Not Buy A New House Before Reading This Shocking Free Report…

- What You Don't Know About Building A New House That Could Cost You Tens-Of-Thousands Of Dollars And Threaten The Financial Livelihood Of Your Family

- 11 Things No Homebuilder Would Dare Tell You Before Taking A Deposit (Number 5 Could Cost You $100,000S)

- 6 Fatal Traps Of Buying A New Home Exposed! The Dirty Little Lies No Real Estate Agent, Builder, Or Even A Buyers Advocate Would Dare Tell You!

So many more people would be compelled to read your ad and get in touch with you for your free report, right?

If you present information that reads like a public service announcement, you're guaranteed to stand out from the crowd in a huge way. Ads like this incentivise prospects, drawing them towards you with the promise of value and, importantly, *no sales pitch.*

The valuable information you're offering here is called a **High-Value Content Offer (HVCO)**, and it draws leads to you like moths to a flame. HVCOs come in multiple forms – free reports, ebooks, videos, cheat sheets – but the goal is always the same: to offer your prospects incredible value, typically in the form of the solution to a problem they're struggling with, without asking them to purchase anything in return. In return for all the value you're providing, all you ask for is their name and email address.

Now you have their attention, you can include information in your report that will move them up the pyramid more quickly. For example, you could get prospects who are still saving money and in research mode to consider buying a new house right away by showing them finance packages that don't require a huge deposit.

IMPORTANT: It's called a High-Value Content Offer for a reason! There not only needs to be *perceived* high value, but it must *deliver* on that promise. When you offer information as an incentive, make sure it's substantive rather than the cheap gibberish that clogs the Internet.

This is the very first exchange of value your prospect makes with your business. They receive the information you have on offer in exchange for providing their contact details.

You can't simply trick people into giving you their contact details and then send them a crappy two-page free 'report' that is simply a promotional piece about your company.

The goal is to wow them with this experience. If done right, this will prompt a conversation to take place in their mind: 'If this is what they're giving away for free, imagine what their paid products/services are like!'

You want to lead with your best foot forward and deliver incredible value.

But first, to stop you from lighting your money on fire, this is what you absolutely must do immediately before creating a HVCO, setting up a website, landing page or running ads of any kind.

Value-Based Marketing

Built on the simple premise of 'giving before asking', value-based marketing is about offering value to your customers without asking for a sale in return.

In my business, we use this in everything we do to create goodwill in the marketplace. Because when you deliver massive value to your prospects, you score a double whammy:

First, your prospects thank you for the materials.

Second, you position yourself as the trusted expert.

So while everyone else is just screaming, 'Buy, buy, buy!' you're building goodwill by showing people you *could* help them... *by actually helping them!*

What's more, with this kind of marketing you're speaking to people who aren't yet ready to buy but who are curious about what you sell. Remember – that's a whopping 97% of prospects!

Most people get this wrong and immediately try to sell to the 97%, but the fact is, fast selling doesn't work with cold traffic. These people have no idea who you are – it's like asking someone to marry you on a first date! We will look at this again later, but for now, remember this rule:

The temperature of your marketing message must match the temperature of your traffic.

Now don't be sceptical. Value-based marketing isn't some

new-fangled strategy or shiny new object. It's just one that's been grossly forgotten. And it's how you'll outsell your competitors – even if you're up against an industry giant and only have a small budget.

Let me tell you a little story...

It's a forgotten case study on how one ad pulled in *three million leads* – and how you can model this strategy to create a stampede of new customers to your own business.

Imagine you do a promotion, you run an ad, and you generate some leads and then some sales... and it's pretty good. But then you go to your mailbox and you open it and find handwritten letters... like, a lot of them! And they say things like, 'God bless you!' and 'I've been searching for this information my entire life!'

And then imagine, you say, gosh... I'm going to run that ad again! And you do, and over time it generates *three million leads* for you and millions of customers.

Guess what? This actually happened! This sales and marketing methodology was conceived in 1948 by a man named Louis Engel.

Engel was a frustrated editor from Jacksonville, Florida. He graduated with a degree in philosophy, had a few jobs, and bounced around a bit as an editor for several organisations. He got fed up with journalism and ended up in a position as an advertising and sales promotion manager for the prestigious Wall Street investment firm of Merrill Lynch, Pierce, Fenner & Beane.

He wasn't a seasoned marketing guy, but he had a crazy idea and suggested to his bosses, 'Instead of running ads telling everybody how great we are, why don't we run an ad and give away some useful information, something that educates our prospects, and then offer to give away some more useful information?'

His bosses replied, 'No, that's a ridiculous idea, and it's not going to work. This is advertising, and we're going to run an ordinary ad'.

They went back and forth, and eventually Engel said, 'Let's just test it, and if it works it works, and if it doesn't I'll go away'.

They said, 'Ok, fine'.

He wrote an ad and they were scared to death of it – it was 6,540 words long and filled an entire full page with tiny six or eight point type!

They said, 'There's no way this thing is going to work'. But they agreed to test it in a small regional newspaper, and in its first week it pulled in 5,000 leads. And this was in 1948, so in order to respond, readers had to clip out some stuff, write their name and details on it, and actually physically post back their information. 5,000 people did this! Engel's bosses said, 'Ok, maybe this guy is onto something'. On October 19, 1948, they published his ad in *The New York Times*.

The good news is that this approach may have been forgotten over the years, but it still works better than probably anything you've seen before. You might be thinking, I don't want to run newspaper ads. Well, the first thing I want you to know is that you can use this strategy for all types of media – on a website or landing page, blog posts, email, Facebook ads, or Google ads.

It begins with a brilliantly-written headline that you could model for your own business, beginning with 'What everybody ought to know about'. This is a great headline because it presupposes that everybody wants to know about the stock and bond business and also assumes there are things you don't know. (Personally, I'd like to split test with the use of numbers – 'The 11 things that everybody ought to know about…')

But this is where it gets really powerful. Because while your competitors are pretending they don't want to sell anything or they're just screaming 'Buy! Buy! Buy!', this ad straight out of the gate addresses reader scepticism by having a box that reads, 'Why are we publishing this information?' The 'This is why' strategy is brilliant and you should model it for your business to increase trust in your marketplace and ultimately your sales.

Naturally, anyone reading anything these days is sceptical, especially online. That box first addresses the deafening scepticism in the reader's mind that asks why they are publishing this information. If they didn't do this, the reader wouldn't be able to concentrate on the content being delivered because they'd be thinking in the back of their mind, 'Why? Why? Why?' and they wouldn't focus on the ad or absorb the message.

It also addresses the pre-established stigma of the stock and bond business being confusing by saying, 'Some plain talk about…'

It then goes onto address well-organised questions the reader already has. Louis Engel likely spoke with analysts at Merrill Lynch to find out their prospects' most common questions, then created subheadlines and bolded each one of them through the ad, which is simply brilliant. Not only did it address reader scepticism but also educated the reader by providing value well in advance of ever asking for the sale or anything in return.

All in all, this isn't great direct response copy – there are no hooks or crazy guarantees or hype, or even a whole bunch of intrigue other than the great headline – just straight up education and value. However, it's still a lead generation ad. We want the reader to take action and do something – and look how masterfully they did exactly that!

By today's standards, the copy isn't spectacular; it's more the overall approach that's so brilliant – the way they phrase the call to action, which of course is, 'Let us know if you want more information'. The call to action (CTA) goes on to say, 'We can't cover everything here as it would take several volumes and naturally you probably have further questions, we'd be glad to send you a copy of this ad in pamphlet form, at no charge, no obligation... just write or phone us'.

This whole approach worked incredibly well and helped make Merrill Lynch a household name far beyond Wall Street.

Now at this stage you might be thinking, yeah this all sounds great Sabri... But no one reads all that copy these days. People have short attention spans.

Really? Let me tell you this....

Only Marketing Morons Believe That No One Reads Long-Form Copy

You might think that no one in today's day and age reads long-form copy. But the truth is, when it comes to making sales, long-form copy will beat short-form copy every single time. I've spent $30 million dollars on generating traffic and running thousands of scientific split tests, and I can tell you without a shadow of doubt that long-form copy works.

With one caveat: The copy must be entertaining and engaging. You can't simply write long copy and think that it's going to make your prospect buy. With that said, when your copy is entertaining, people won't care how long it is.

You might still be saying, 'But who reads all that text?'

The **buyers** are the ones who read it. They are the ones who have all the burning questions, the ones who are looking for answers. The people who aren't going to read your copy aren't going to buy in any case. So would you rather gear your copy towards those who are never going to buy, or would you rather convert more of the people who are deep in research mode, genuinely interested in buying, and looking to be pushed over the edge? The answer should be very, very simple.

The approach used by Merrill Lynch was brilliantly

effective for several reasons: it created goodwill in their marketplace by giving something of value away for free before ever asking for anything. Over the years, this approach has been reskinned and renamed many times, from permission-based marketing to content marketing. However, it's not the name or the specific tactics that you should be concerned with, rather the overarching strategy that makes it so effective.

You see, it appeals to the exact segment of the market you want because your message rises above the noise that's created by loudness, hype, and the general lameness of your competition. If all your marketing consists of you screaming, *'Buy my stuff!'* then you're only appealing to a fraction of your potential buyers and you're missing out on a huge percentage of the total number of potential buyers in your market.

This is a great reminder that the job of an ad is not to sell but to *create intrigue* and get the prospect to raise their hand and say, 'I'm interested'.

Why this approach is so much more effective than what everyone else is doing

There are three ways we can influence people:

- Talk about how good we are.

- Have others talk about how good we are.

- *Demonstrate* how good we are.

In sales and marketing, #3 is the most effective.

Demonstrating how good you are doesn't only help with influencing them, but it creates heaps of goodwill and helps you reach a much larger segment of your market, like it did with Merrill Lynch. And let's not forget, people are 10 times more likely to come to you to learn something than they are to be sold to.

So, using the approach gleaned from Merrill Lynch's ad that generated over three million leads, we can take the information and answers we know our prospect is craving for, and package it as a **High-Value Content Offer (HVCO).**

You can see in the graphic below, a scenario that doesn't involve anything more complicated than some simple third grade math....

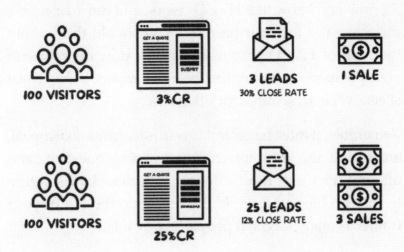

The above graph represents two different scenarios:

Scenario 1: You send 100 people to a website or landing page that is speaking only to the 3% of your market who are looking to buy, with a call to action (CTA) like 'get a quote'. This type of CTA typically converts at around 3%, resulting in the three leads. A typical conversion rate for this type of offer generally converts at 30%, resulting in this exercise yielding one sale.

Scenario 2: You send the same 100 people to a website or landing page that speaks to the burning questions that market has with a HVCO. This type of offer generally converts at 25% because it's aimed at educating the market rather than selling. Because the offer is more educational, naturally there is less buyer intent behind it, so these leads close at a lower rate of typically around 12% if nurtured correctly. Resulting in three sales. Net result? Same cost to generate the 100 visitors, with *triple* the amount of sales.

So, now you know that HVCOs work, and can *dramatically* increase sales for your business, you should think about the type of HVCO that would really provide value for your prospects, whether that be a free report, video, cheat sheet, webinar, seminar, or otherwise.

Remember, it must be geared towards mass market appeal, answering the most prominent burning question, and offering the single most valuable and immediate solution to that problem. All while drawing into the top of your funnel as many targeted people as possible.

Now let's get into the actual mechanics on how to create an HVCO for your business.

There are three rules you must follow when putting together the kind of HVCO that will explode your sales:

HVCO Rule #1: Create an Attention-Grabbing Headline

HVCO Rule #2: Make sure every point touches a burning issue.

HVCO Rule #3: Keep it simple.

Now, they're all important, and we'll come to rules #2 & #3 in a moment; but first, the single most critical part of this process is having an attention-grabbing headline that stops your prospects in their tracks, grabs them by the throat, and creates so much intrigue that it practically forces them to give you their contact details.

HVCO Rule #1: Create An Attention-Grabbing Headline

To illustrate the importance and power of this, let me share a short story. In 1982, Naura Hayden released a book called *Astro-Logical Love*.

Looking at the title, what do you think this book is about? Does it grab you and demand your attention? Is it clear and specific as to what you'll learn?

Well, when they print a book, the first print run is typically 5,000 books, and most books don't sell out in their first run. This book also didn't sell out in the initial 5,000. In fact, it sold only 2,000 copies.

So Hayden sold the rest of her books to discount book stores and flea marketers who sell books for 99 cents. It was there that a New York publisher stumbled across the book, bought it, read it, and thought, 'This is a great book about how to seduce women'.

He called Naura Hayden and bought the rights to the book and republished it. *He didn't change one word inside the book.*

Exact same book… The product was the same.

But he changed the title to this: *How to Satisfy a Woman Every Time… and Have Her Beg for More!*

Which book would you rather read if you were in the market for that type of thing?

Well, the result was 2.3 million books sales in the first 18 months!

It became a massive cultural phenomenon and a New York Times #1 best seller. Same book, same content, just a different title. It wasn't the picture on the cover that made the difference (actually there is no picture). It was the title, and more specifically the offer in the title that changed.

And that was an offer that someone actually wanted. The take-away for you is simple and clear:

Identify your Dream Buyer's single most pervasive and persistent hair-on-fire problem – and then offer them the single most valuable and immediate solution.

Once you're clear on this, really labour over figuring out the best possible title for your free report. Because the truth is, the title of your free report is the number one factor in the pulling power of your HVCO and will largely be responsible for the amount of people that enter your funnel… and the amount of sales you make.

Like the example earlier, you don't want to call your free report How to Make Men Want You. It's a vanilla offer and it doesn't intrigue the reader. You want to name it, Make Him Beg to Be Your Boyfriend in Six Simple Steps.

Consider an HVCO that King Kong put together: 22 Money Murdering Mistakes That No Web Designer Would Dare Tell You. It's a lot more compelling than Five Things You Should Know When Building Your Website. We dialled up the volume, using strong imagery that provoked a visceral response. You want to make your title burn with intrigue and be absolutely irresistible

- If the title of your HVCO isn't enticing and doesn't stop people in their tracks, then nobody's going to download it. And if nobody downloads it, you'll have nobody entering the top of your funnel and you'll have nobody to call. You'll have no leads and you'll make no sales.

- Having a really good title to your HVCO literally pulls everybody into the top of the funnel.

So, how do you get people to actually read your stuff? Here are five headline essentials:

HEADLINE ESSENTIAL #1 – YOU NEED A HEADLINE THAT GRABS THEM AND PRACTICALLY FORCES THEM TO READ YOUR MATERIAL

"On average, five times as many people read the headline as read the body copy. When you've written your headline, you've spent eighty cents out of your dollar".

- David Ogilvy

People who write copy and craft headlines and ads for a living are called copywriters. And which publications have the highest-paid copywriters on the planet? You might think it's a huge advertising agency, or maybe Coca-Cola, or Nike, but you'd be wrong.

The answer is gossip magazines and news publications. Like *Women's Weekly*, *AARP* and *The National Enquirer*.

For those wondering what The National Enquirer is, it's one of those trashy gossip magazines in the US that you see near the checkout in supermarkets and convenience stores. But there's a good reason why they pay their copywriters so much. The writers for *The National Enquirer* are among the best anywhere on earth. I'm not being sarcastic. They really are. If you doubt that, here's something for you to consider.

Approximately seven million people read *The National Enquirer* each and every week! Enquirer articles are superbly written. They are clear, concise, crisp, and, all in all, the most easily understood articles of any publication. And what do *Enquirer* writers excel at above all else?

You guessed it – HEADLINES. Their headlines are so powerful and have so much grabbing power that every week, people who've sworn they'll never again buy such a publication are almost forced to purchase it despite themselves.

Let's take a quick look at the attention-grabbing pulling power of their headlines now.

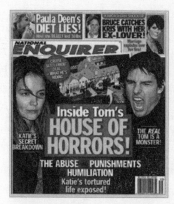

Look at the wording: 'Exposed!' 'Revealed!' 'Confession!' 'Horror!' 'Secret!' 'Torture!'

These are all emotional trigger words that strike up very visceral emotions. Now at this stage you might be thinking, 'I could never position my business as these trashy mags do!'

Slow down. Be patient and stay with me.

It's not just the *National Enquirer* that does this. Let's look at something a little closer to home and see what we can learn about how to create an irresistible, attention-grabbing headline.

Take a moment to look at each one of these covers and see if you can see some commonalities, other than of course all being fixated on 'Better Sex!' and 'Getting Chiselled Six-Pack Abs!' Something else should jump out at you, something that adds to the grabbing power of their headline. Let's take the first one, *Glamour Magazine* with Jennifer Lopez on the cover. Notice the use of numbers...

HEADLINE ESSENTIAL #2: NUMBERS

Numbers give your prospects a tangible object or logical idea to wrap their head around. They also lay out a structure the reader instantly knows will be easy to follow (not forgetting it makes it easier for you to write). Would you rather read '5 things you must know before hiring a wedding planner' or 'Some helpful information about hiring a wedding planner'? The answer should be obvious.

So, let's try it for your business:

- '7 Things You Must Know Before Hiring a Financial Planner'

- '12 Things No Wedding Photographer Would Tell You'

- '22 Money Murdering Mistakes No Web Designer Would Dare Tell You'

It doesn't matter what industry you're in, this is cut and paste: 'Shocking reporting reveals the 5 things you *must* know about X'.

I've used it in hundreds of industries and it's never not worked.

Remember, your prospects are more distracted than ever before. People browsing the web are basically sleepwalkers and you must jolt them awake like an electric shock. Remember, they're only one click away from seductive porn or irresistibly cute cat videos.

In the first few seconds you must grab them by the throat and drag them into your copy and your offer. Once you have their attention with an attention-grabbing headline, this sets you up for the 'meat and bones' of your ad where you need to create enough desire for them to give you their contact details and download your HVCO – and therefore enter your funnel. And you do that by creating irresistible intrigue.

HEADLINE ESSENTIAL #3: CREATE IRRESISTIBLE INTRIGUE

It's not enough just to get their attention and sell the benefits of your offer. You also need to pique your reader's interest and have them burning with curiosity. The best way to do that is to dial up the intrigue.

A great way to create irresistible intrigue is by using words such as 'Must', 'Alarming', 'Shocking', 'Won't Tell You', 'Exposed!' 'Revealed' 'Confession!' 'Horror' 'Secret'. *You can download an additional list of power words to help you get started at https://resources.selllikecrazy.co/*

Or try adding a twist or qualifier to the hook, i.e., 'How to start and scale an online business, even if you don't know what to sell'. By adding the 'even if you don't know what to sell' it not only qualifies people who don't know what they want to sell, but also increases the intrigue for your prospect to find out how that's possible.

HEADLINE ESSENTIAL #4: SHOW THEM WHAT'S IN IT FOR THEM

Your HVCO should ultimately be about them and their desired outcome. Your prospect needs (and wants) an immediate benefit and the key is to write about *them* – not you.

Show them how they'll learn simple tips that will help solve their problem. Show them what their desired outcome looks like, and then educate them on how to get there. That's the payoff the reader gets in exchange for their email address.

You must add as many specific and vivid details as possible. Let's look at one of the titles for a free report we looked at earlier:

'7 Things You Must Know Before Hiring a Financial Planner'

That's already better than most. Most people would generally go with something very vague like:

'7 Things to Know About Financial Planning'

How can we juice this up and make it more irresistible?

Lets add in some power words.

'7 Alarming Things You Must Know Before Hiring A Financial Planner'

'7 Shocking Things You Must Know Before Hiring A Financial Planner'

'7 Horrors You Must Know Before Hiring A Financial Planner'

That's a bit better, but what else can we do to really get these singing?

Well, one more thing we can do to take these titles to the next level is to make them as specific and bursting with intrigue as possible.

'7 Horrors You Must Know Before Hiring a Financial Planner (Not knowing these could cost you $10,000s!)'

'7 Alarming Things You Must Know Before Hiring A Financial Planner (#3 Will Blow Your Mind!)'

That last one is strong. The intrigue has been dialled up. Let's go with that.

FINALLY REVEALED...

7 Alarming Things You Must Know Before Hiring A Financial Planner

(#3 Will Blow Your Mind!)

Top financial planner reveals his secret checklist and the dirty little lies that could cost you $10,000s and stop you from retiring 7 years early. Shocking free report reveals all!

Now let's take a step back and compare the original title with the one we've just created:

'7 Things to Know About Financial Planning'

vs.

'7 Alarming Things You Must Know Before Hiring a Financial Planner (#3 Will Blow Your Mind!)'

Which sounds more compelling? More intriguing? Which would more likely to convince you to hand over your contact details in exchange for that info?

BORING

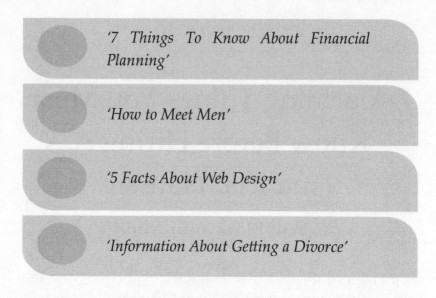

'7 Things To Know About Financial Planning'

'How to Meet Men'

'5 Facts About Web Design'

'Information About Getting a Divorce'

IRRESISTIBLE

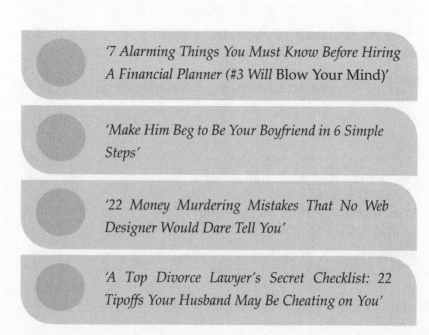

'7 Alarming Things You Must Know Before Hiring A Financial Planner (#3 Will Blow Your Mind)'

'Make Him Beg to Be Your Boyfriend in 6 Simple Steps'

'22 Money Murdering Mistakes That No Web Designer Would Dare Tell You'

'A Top Divorce Lawyer's Secret Checklist: 22 Tipoffs Your Husband May Be Cheating on You'

Timeless Formulas For Your HVCO Titles

Timeless Formula #1

X ways to achieve **[Desirable Thing]** without doing **[Undesirable Thing]**

Example:

6 Ways to Get Washboard Abs Without Doing a Single Sit -Up

Timeless Formula #2

[Do Difficult Thing] in [Specific Period of Time] Even if [Shortcomings]

Example:

Pay Off Your Mortgage in 7 Years Even if You Have a Modest Income

Timeless Formula #3

Achieve **[Desirable Thing]** like **[An Expert]** Even Without [Something Expected]

Example:

Paint Masterpieces Like Picasso Without Ever Having a Single Lesson!

Timeless Formula #4

How to Eliminate **[Biggest Problem]** without doing **[The Thing They Hate]** Within **[Specific Timeframe]**

Example:

How to Eliminate Your Muffin Top Without Giving Up the Foods You Love – Within 21 Days or Less!

These are all pretty good starting points for your HVCO title. They speak to your prospect's needs in a clear and concise way.

You don't need to reinvent the wheel every time you write a new report. However, if you can come up with a unique and memorable title, it will suck in leads like a vacuum cleaner on steroids.

HCVO Tip #2: Make Sure Every Point Touches A Burning Issue

Make sure every point in your HVCO touches on a burning question your audience has. If you're writing a report or an ebook, do this in the sub-heads to ensure anyone just skimming it will get pulled in.

For example, if your headline is this:

'5 Shocking Ways Internet Thieves Are Stealing Your Private Data – And the Secrets to Protecting Your Family!'

Every point or subhead in the text needs to support this assertion. For example, a subhead could be:

'#1 – Think Your Password Keeps You Safe? Think Again!'

And,

'#2 –Destructive Malware Will Fry Your Computer!'

The point is that if you make an assertion in your title or headline, you must back it up in the text. Keep up the pressure!

HCVO Tip #3: Keep It Simple

Start by writing a free report or ebook. There are lots of different types of HVCOs (see below for a list), but reports and ebooks are easy to create, and you can have one up and sucking in leads in no time. All you have to do is write a short report (5-6 pages is plenty) and convert it into a PDF. (Don't let the simplicity fool you into thinking they're not effective. Some of the most popular HVCOs I've ever deployed were only eight pages.)

You don't even have to write your report from scratch. You could compile your most popular blog posts into one easy-to-digest guide, jazz it up with basic styling, and convert it into a PDF.

Or you could interview experts on a subject, compile the answers into a report, write an irresistible title, and away you go. (Many experts are happy to do this as long as you provide a link back to their business).

HVCO Types

- FREE Consultation
- Coupons
- Checklists
- Cheat sheets
- Quizzes
- Videos
- Video course
- Toolkit
- Calendar
- Podcast
- Interview
- Live demo
- Tickets
- Email course
- Physical product
- Swipe file
- Infographic
- Phone call
- Assessment

- Custom pricing
- White paper
- Ebook
- T-Shirt
- Industry statistics
- Case study
- 'How-to' guide
- PDF download
- Webinar
- E Course

Zoom webs

Action Points

- Using the comments and concerns you discovered in Phase 1, brainstorm a HVCO you can produce to answer the questions keeping your ideal customer up at night.

- Choose your best idea and create a solid High-Value Content Offer (a free report, video or cheat sheet, etc.) that gets your dream buyer to raise their hands and identify themselves as being interested in what you're selling. The content and title of this HVCO should address the #1 most common 'hair on fire' question or concern your market is having and that kept coming up from your research. The HVCO should be positioned to solve that problem or answer that question.

- Ensure your copy contains a bold headline and a strong call to action.

- Speak to your audience in the same language as the questions they're asking.

- Don't be afraid to directly address how your products and services fill the gap.

When you connect with your audience this way, you'll resonate on a far more influential level. In fact, your customers will feel as if your products or services are tailored specifically for their exact needs and desires, making this the most effective way to grow your business.

PHASE 3:

Capture Leads And Get Contact Details

This is where I see 99% of businesses getting it wrong. They approach their prospects like an army would attack a walled city - with a full frontal assault. They send traffic straight to a landing page, or even worse, their homepage, and attempt to go straight for the sale and pray they'll make a profit.

They simply disregard all the necessary steps that take place to turn a stranger into a satisfied, paying client. They are far too eager to make a sales pitch. They make the wrong assumption and treat everybody in their market as if they're already eager to buy.

No wining, no dining... *nothing*! They are doing the equivalent of walking into a bar and asking a stranger to marry them!

As discussed already, we must follow a proven process in order to turn strangers into high-paying clients; and the next step in this process is to get them to 'opt-in'.

Yes, the single purpose of the opt-in page is just that: to get people to give you their contact details in exchange for what it is you're 'selling', typically a HVCO.

'Selling' in quotes is not a typo. I use the term 'selling' even though you will be giving this away for free. Why? Well, this *is the very first transaction* that takes place between you and your prospect. While there may be no exchange of money, the currency in which they're paying for this piece of information consists of their name and email address. And you must wow them. If you're simply handing them a crappy promotional report about how great your products and services are, you'll lose all trust and will be pedalling uphill from the very beginning.

Just because you're not collecting cash for your free report doesn't mean you shouldn't make it the type of quality someone would happily pay money for. The information you're giving away on your opt-in page must be so good that it leaves your prospects saying, 'If they're giving away such valuable content for free, imagine what their paid products and services are like!'

So, what should you put on an opt-in page to make it so irresistible and bursting with so much intrigue that it practically forces visitors to quickly cough up their contact details in exchange for what you're offering?

Well, the good news is that we've already done the heavy lifting when we completed the Halo Strategy and uncovered your market's deepest pains, fears, hopes and dreams. This is where you can use this information to hit your prospects' hot buttons to motivate them to opt-in for your HVCO.

Everything You Need To Create A Killer Opt-In Page

When building your opt-in page, you should include these elements:

- A headline that grabs your reader by the throat.

- A subheadline that restates your offer and what they're getting.

- Ultra-compelling fascination bullets: Short and punchy explanation of how the content is going to help your prospect and make sure they're oozing with intrigue.

- A visual representation of what they're getting – a free report, cheat sheet, etc.

- A basic form for people to enter their name and email to access the content.

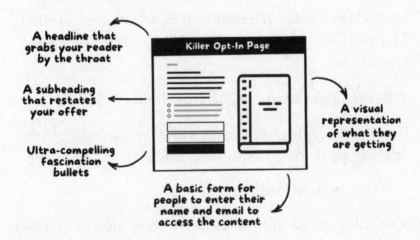

The Opt-In Headline

The headline should snap your reader's eyeballs to the screen and promise them a specific, vivid benefit. Focus on solving one specific pain point for your prospect. If it's too vague it will roll over your prospects like water off a duck's back. It should focus on your prospect's exact needs and then offer an immediate solution to their problem.

When you're writing opt-in copy, you've got to have

energy behind it. Turn up the volume and take it to the extreme. Why?

People browsing online are basically sleepwalking zombies. They roam from site to site until they find something that strikes them. Your copy must be like a thundering bolt of lightning that shoots through their bodies and shocks them awake from their slumber.

To do this you must turn up the volume *full blast*.

Headline Formula:

Finally! How to Get [DESIRED RESULT] Without [THING THEY FEAR MOST] in [SPECIFIC TIME FRAME] - Guaranteed.

'[PROBLEM]? Get My [SOLUTION] and [RESULT]'

If you're struggling to come up with a unique headline, this little puppy works a treat, every, single, time. Guaranteed.

The Opt-In SubHeadline

The subheadline simply restates your offer and what they're specifically getting, such as this: '26-page Paleo cookbook including 16 delicious Paleo-friendly recipes you can make in under 20 minutes PLUS beautiful high-resolution pictures'.

It should then go on to explain how this will be delivered, and leave nothing to question, such as: 'Simply enter your email address below and a PDF copy will instantly be sent right to your inbox'.

Ultra-Compelling Fascination Bullets

Bullet copy or fascination bullets are small nuggets of tantalising teaser information that intrigue the reader while offering or implying a benefit. They're designed to crank up the curiosity of your prospect and make not opting-in virtually impossible. It's what can give that last nudge required to push your prospect over the edge.

The number one thing that impacts the effectiveness of your bullets?

It's curiosity.

'Curiosity', said the legendary American advertising pioneer Claude Hopkins, 'is among the strongest of human incentives'.

So instead of barraging prospects with blatant benefits, you want to craft bullet copy that teases, tantalises, and tempts prospects — intensifying their curiosity to almost unbearable levels, and then inviting them to satisfy that curiosity for free, simply by opting in.

Writing great fascinations is an art form demanding a great eye, well-developed skill, and tremendous creativity. It's an endeavour that can take years to master.

To circumvent this arduous task, I've included my *fascination bullet copy formulas* for writing compelling bullet copy in minutes.

Fascination Bullet Copy Formulas

How to X without Y: 'How to get washboard abs without doing a single sit-up'. 'How to meet single men without speed dating or hanging out in bars'. 'How to invest in real estate with no money down'.

You need X, right? Wrong! Address a common belief and then create massive curiosity by talking against it. 'Drinking 3 litres of water a day is healthy, right? WRONG!'

'Discover the number one thing you can do to stay 20 times more hydrated than drinking water'. This creates massive intrigue.

X ways to Y: This is the most classic of all, 'Five ways to meet single women in Melbourne'. Classic, straight forward copy.

Where to find Y: 'Where to find the most ravenous hyperactive buyers online'.

How to eliminate X: 'How to stop joint pain forever'. 'How to never pay another cent in tax'.

What you should never: This is a great one, as people are more compelled to know what they shouldn't do than what they should. Fear of loss (pain) is greater than fear of attainment (joy).

'What you should never say to a woman on your first date'. 'What you should never do when trying to win over a prospect'.

Say goodbye to X [frustration]: 'Say goodbye to calorie counting and hour-long cardio sessions'.

The truth about Y: 'The dirty truth about fish oil revealed'. 'The truth about flossing only after you've brushed your teeth'.

Have you been doing X wrong? (And does it really matter?) 'Have you been boiling your eggs in the wrong pot? (And does it really matter?)'

'Show, Don't Tell': Visually Represent the Value of the Opt-In

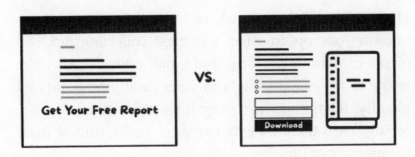

It's not enough to just tell your prospects about what they're going to get. You need to *show* them, and make it polished so the perceived value is very high. Just the same way an online shopper wouldn't buy something online without seeing high-resolution images, your prospects will be reluctant to hand over their contact details without seeing what they're getting.

If it's a free report or ebook, show them a physical book or brochure mock-up. If it's a cheat sheet, show them how many pages they are getting.

Collect Their Name and Email Address

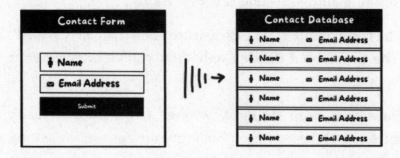

Don't *ask* them, *tell them* where to put their contact details to get the mouth-watering content you're offering in exchange.

The less information you ask for, the higher the conversion rate on your opt-in page. I suggest collecting just two pieces of data: their name and email address. All we're trying to get our prospects to do is raise their hand and identify themselves as being interested in what we're selling. We'll then use email automation to nurture these prospects over time.

Here are a few real-life examples:

NOTICE:

- It's crystal clear this offer is aimed at people looking for a childcare centre.

- The use of numbers.

- Answers the top questions in that market: How will my child fit in at a childcare centre? What should I be looking for in a childcare centre?

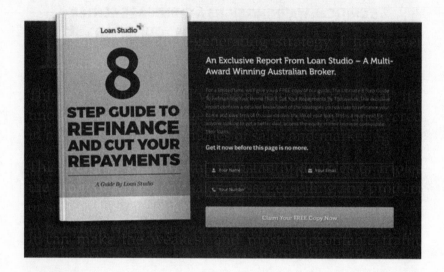

Discover How To Refinance Your Home And SLASH Your Loan Repayments By Thousands

Our Exclusive 8 Step Guide Makes It Easy And Profitable To Get A Better Deal On Your Mortgage Today

NOTICE:

- It's crystal clear this offer is aimed at people looking for refinance.

- The use of numbers.

- Answers the top questions in that market: How can I best refinance my home? What should I be looking for?

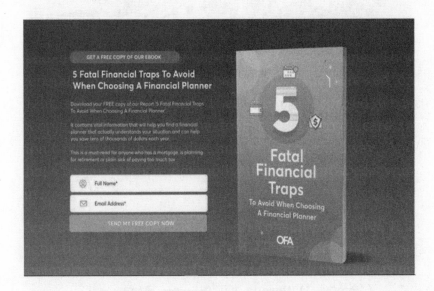

NOTICE:

- It's crystal clear this is aimed at people looking for a financial planner.

- The use of numbers.

- Answers the top questions in that market: How do I find a decent financial planner? What should I be looking out for?

NOTICE:

- It's crystal clear it's aimed at people looking to be healthier, and the method is by consuming green smoothies.

- The use of numbers.

- Answers the number top questions in that market: How do I get healthier? How do I make tasty and different green smoothies?

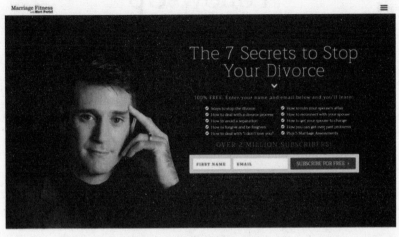

NOTICE:

- It's crystal this offer is aimed at married people who don't want to get divorced.

- The use of numbers.

- Answers the top questions in that market: How do I avoid a divorce? How can I improve my marriage?

Follow-Up

Now we've used a HVCO to appeal to the largest percentage of your market and collected their contact details via our opt-in page, we now have the ability to follow up and nurture these prospects via email and make them offers (that is where the majority of the sales will be made).

But right now, we have the opportunity to capture the 'hyper-active buyers' – by making them an offer so good they can't refuse – using a technique called The Godfather Strategy which we'll cover in the next chapter.

You see, once a prospect downloads your HVCO they will automatically be redirected to a thank you page, which we'll be using as a landing page to make your Godfather offer.

PHASE 4:

The Godfather Strategy

This is the single most powerful, most effective, and most profit-generating strategy I have ever discovered....

This is the one secret I've been reluctant to reveal. It's unquestionably the biggest secret I have ever uncovered in my 17 years in the trenches of sales and marketing.

This secret is so powerful, it instantly doubles or triples the profit of almost any sales message, selling any product or service in any market.

It can make the weakest and most unprofitable traffic sources into your own personal t of the most ravenous and 'itchy-to-buy' customers available.

It's my secret weapon. And it has allowed me to invade and conquer multiple industries in multiple markets with multiple businesses and crush much more established competitors into a fine powder that scatters in the wind.

This is the Godfather Strategy:

Make Your Prospects An Offer They Can't Refuse

Simple, isn't it?

An 'offer' consists of two things:

- What your prospects want when they respond to your marketing.

- What they have to do to get it.

And it's where 99% of businesses get it wrong. They generate leads, or, if they have their head screwed on right, offer a free report. Then they're surprised when people don't show up at the door waving a credit card, or don't whip out their wallet and buy straight away. And that's because they're not motivating their prospects with an *irresistible offer*.

Less than 1% of the businesses I consult with have this right before I work with them. They don't have any resemblance of an irresistible offer. Instead, they are using *resistible offers* and wonder why their business is stuck.

The Godfather Strategy is about making an irresistible offer with balls. It's about making some huge claims and some big promises. It's about having an offer so white hot that it melts objections and obliterates any friction between you and the sale... and... almost *forces* your prospects to buy.

Sadly, what I see all the time is that most business owners start in a position of *weakness*. Their promises are weak and watered down.

They have no resemblance of a compelling offer. Instead they have an impotent offer that looks something like this: 'Use our service and you might see some sort of benefit sometime in the distant future'. Or, 'Download this free report, and we'll tell you how great it is to have our products and services'.

These horrible, weak, and frail offers are simply not good enough to withstand the competitive gale force winds that rage through online marketplaces.

Here is how you create a hair-raising offer that stops your prospects in their tracks and demands their attention and practically forces them to buy.

Grab a cup of coffee or tea and get comfortable. Because unless your offers are already radically different from the tens of thousands of businesses I've seen, we're about to add big bucks to your bottom line.

The One Unbreakable Rule Of Marketing That Can Ensure Your Success

In the old days, merchants and customers hammered out most purchases face-to-face in the town square. The merchant yelled out their offers, the buyer haggled for the best price, and asked the merchant to sweeten the pot by adding something extra or discounting the price.

The advent of mass marketing changed all that, of course. Today, digital consumers are accustomed to having your best offer presented to them on demand, with little to no human interaction.

Things have become incredibly fragmented.

With every passing day, our prospects are exposed to ever-more-amazing offers – especially on the Internet.

So the very first step in the process is this:

Sell What People Want To Buy

This might sound elementary, but you wouldn't believe how many supposedly smart, university-educated people in business don't understand this.

They start by looking at what they would like to buy, and not their market. They swim against the raging river that is the desires of their marketplace and begin with their own interests in mind. They ask, 'What would I like to buy? What is convenient for me to sell? What do I think is a cool gizmo or service?'

They don't ask, *'What is the market starving for?'*

Once you've done your research using the Halo Strategy and have discovered what people *really* want in your market, then sell it to them!

Keep in mind that sometimes you can have the right crowd at the wrong time. You could be offering the best hamburgers in the world, but if you're trying to sell those hamburgers to a crowd that has just finished a seven-course gourmet meal, you won't have many customers.

If, through this process, you uncover that what you're selling isn't indeed what your market is starving for, don't try and put lipstick on a pig. That is, don't try and dress up what you're selling as being what they want and try and fool yourself or your market.

Do not try and reason with or convince yourself that what you're selling is 'good enough'.

Good enough won't cut it. Simply do what's required in order to pivot your business to align with what your market desires most. Fire employees, get rid of departments, sell the remainder of your stock in a fire sale. Whatever it is, do it. *Do not flog a dead horse.*

Enduring short-term hardship, loss, or discomfort will save you a lot of extreme long-term pain.

Most business owners and entrepreneurs spend tens of thousands of dollars developing a product or service *before* they've done deep market research or put together their offer or sales message.

They then try and mould their sales pitch to fit what their product and service can actually do, removing this claim or promise, or that benefit, ultimately castrating the sales message from the get-go.

The right way to approach this is to write your sales message *before* ever creating the product and service. Make the biggest claims, give the market what they're starving for, create the dream-come-true experience for your market. And then, and only then, start to develop the product or service to deliver on it.

Moving on: Once you know what your market is starving for, then you take your product or service and craft it into a compelling pitch … an *offer they can't refuse*.

Here's how you do it.

Create A Detail Sheet: Features And Benefits

First, create a 'Detail Sheet' about the product or services you want to sell. On this sheet you should have two columns, column one should be titled 'Features' and this is where you list the *full* list of the features of what you are selling.

The second column should be titled 'Benefits'. This column is where you convert all the features into corresponding benefits.

Don't discount the importance of this just because it sounds simple. While this might sound very simple, if you do this exercise correctly and do a good job on your research, your offers will almost write themselves.

IMPORTANT: Please ensure you take a lot of time with this. Really sweat over it. Most amateur marketers and rookie copywriters don't do this step at all, and even most of the 'top' copywriters don't labour nearly long enough over it.

You should literally list every single feature about what you are selling that you can possibly think of.

Once you're finished with this step and your Detail Sheet is as comprehensive as you can make it, we are now ready for part two which is to write a Benefit List.

What we do here is go over our Detail Sheet and we

translate each feature into a corresponding benefit, wherever possible. So first, lets get clear on the differences of a feature and a benefit. A **feature** is simply a detail or specification. Like the fact your mattress is made from latex, or that it comes in a cotton sleeve.

A **benefit** is what your product *will do for the buyer*. Let's say the mattress on your bed is made from high-grade natural certified latex. That's a *feature*. That fact could translate to *benefits* including it moulds itself to your body for perfect comfort, and it absorbs the movements of a fidgety partner and makes for more undisturbed sleep.

But there could be even *more* benefits! Thanks to the high-grade natural certified latex, you will sleep more soundly, awaken refreshed, perform better during the day at work, get the promotion you wanted, make more money, and move into a bigger house in a nicer neighbourhood.

All because you bought the right mattress.

Here are more examples of how facts and features can translate into benefits:

FEATURE	BENEFIT
• *High-grade natural certified latex*	• *Reduces shoulder and hip pressure* • *Good ventilation* • *Allergy-free properties* • *Allows better blood circulation* • *Provides pressure relief*
• *100% Organic Bamboo Cotton Sheets*	• *Durable and long lasting (will save you money)*
• *Made from breathable material*	• *Keep you cool in the summer and warm in the winter*

If you do this process properly you should have several pages of features and corresponding benefits.

Create Your Offer

Next, start thinking about your offer. Your offer is your basic business proposition, and is by far the most important element in your entire sales message.

Offer Basics

What are you selling? _____

How much does it cost? _____

Who will take immediate action on this offer? _____

How do you claim/buy it? _____

First up, forget about your lawyer. Forget about your industry regulations, and all of that stuff for now. I want you to think about what promise or offer you'd make if you had a magic wand and there were no rules or limitations to what you could say, what you could promise, and what you could have in your offer.

Even if it's not your whole service, even if it's a splinter of your core product or service, what could you give prospects that would give them some results right away? Get creative with it. Really think about what your best offer could possibly be.

I want you to come up with the most powerful offer you can put down in writing. It should be no more than a few lines. When you're doing this, it's really important to remember that no one is going to see this piece of paper except for you at the beginning. This really gives you an opportunity to go over the top and go all out. We want that.

Make it outrageous.

Now it's down on paper, start pulling it back to something that you can actually back up and deliver on and that won't get you sued for false advertising. Obviously, you have to offer only what you can deliver on. Otherwise, that promise is going to backfire and cause all types of headaches and problems for you. You want to start really big, put it down on paper, then dial it back to something that's irresistible but you're still confident you could deliver on.

Irresistible offers are detailed and specific. Let me explain.

Let's say we're selling mattresses online. Let's look at a lacklustre offer I found by doing a quick Google search. (And generally, when we do Google searches, it's very rare that people have great offers, which is why it's no surprise so many businesses fail.) Here's the offer I found:

'Buy your mattress online. Fast and free delivery'.

There was also this restatement of the offer:

'American-made with free delivery. Buy your mattress online today for better quality'. If we reduce that down to this: *'Buy an American-made mattress online with free and fast delivery',* then most people looking at that would think it's okay.

But when you know a thing or two about creating winning offers, you understand that this is an incredibly boring offer. Let's compare this vague and watered down offer to a winning offer in this space.

Take Casper a mattress in a box start-up. This is their offer:

'Get America's best-reviewed mattress, delivered to your door for free, for a 120-night trial'.

This is an irresistible offer that helped Casper shake up a stale $29 billion mattress industry, taking them from zero dollars as a small start-up to over $600 million in sales in their first 4 years of business. That's the power of an irresistible offer.

There's specificity in it. There's risk reversal. And you're going out into the market with a really, really strong and compelling Godfather Offer. If you're in the market for a high-quality mattress, this is an offer that will get you to sit up in your chair. It will raise the hairs on the back of your neck, and it will demand that you pay attention.

And pay attention they did. Their mattress has over 45,000 reviews at the time of this writing, with almost 30,000 of them five-star. Here's another example. Let's say we're a homebuilding company. Again, I've done a quick Google search to see what kind of offers people are running in that market. This is a very important thing to do. You want to see the environment your offer is going to be competing in. In this instance, we're looking at Google Ads. Here we see:

'Home Builders Melbourne. Explore our latest designs. Designing luxury homes from a range of elegant designs. Enquire Now!'

That's their 'offer'. When we reduce it down to a straight headline it turns out it's this: *'Designing luxury homes from a range of elegant designs'*. For most people that sounds pretty good. That's what they do. They design luxury homes. They've got a whole range of elegant designs you can choose from. However, again, this is incredibly vague. It's gutless, and it will be ignored in a sea of other lame, impotent offers that provoke zero action. As a consumer, I don't even know what they want me to do from this. But it certainly doesn't get me excited.

Compare this to an offer we created for home building start-up Enso Homes:

'We'll build your new home in just 30 weeks or give you $5,000 in cash'.

We didn't just create this offer out of thin air. We found from our research (during the Halo Strategy) that the biggest pain point for consumers commissioning boutique luxury homes was that builders often drag out projects and constantly miss deadlines. And we found that most consumers who are building a new home with a boutique builder are renting, and they really can't afford to be renting and doubling up on paying repayments on their house and land plus their rental property for an extended period of time. This was the problem keeping them up at night.

So we created this offer and put it front and centre of all the digital marketing we were doing for Enso Homes. On the website, on the landing pages, in their HVCO. Everywhere. How did it go? Let me tell you how it went. This offer took Enso Homes from zero dollars, and never receiving a deposit ever on a new home build, to over $7 million dollars in revenue in their first eight months. It went nuts. Completely crazy. And that, again, just illustrates what a really compelling offer has when it addresses those specific pain points of that marketplace.

Let's do one more exercise – a little bit closer to home. Let's jump onto Google and look at SEO agencies. This is an offer I found:

'Best SEO management. Digital marketing experts'.

There's no offer here. It's more of a statement, right? There's no specificity, no risk reversal, no timeframes, no end benefit to me. This dull-as-dishwater copy will never awaken your prospects from their sleepy state, shoot an electric thunderbolt through them, nor provoke them to take action. This doesn't get you excited in any way. And this from a company who apparently are digital marketing experts! Now let's take a look at what a winning offer in this space looks like. This is one from yours truly:

'Guaranteed Google rankings in 90 days or we work for free'.

Woo-ee! Now that is an offer. It's bold. It's specific. And it's got risk reversal all over it. Obviously, if we couldn't deliver on that, we'd be quickly going out of business. But when we looked at creating and guaranteeing our offer, we did the research. We found that two-thirds of our target businesses had been with another agency and had been burned because they didn't see the results that they wanted. When they came to us, they were highly sceptical – not necessarily of us, but of the industry as a whole. In response, we wanted to craft an irresistible offer that addressed these pain points, reversed that risk, and really allowed us to guarantee our clients' results.

This offer really helped us invade and conquer our hyper-competitive industry. The waters are bloody from fierce competition in our space. There are *thousands* of digital marketing agencies in Australia. And it's really taken King Kong from my bedroom, with no funding and no venture capital, to being ranked the 28th fastest-growing company in Australia by the *Australian Financial Review* two years in a row. And also the fastest-growing digital agency in the country. That's the kind of power that a potent offer has.

Your Offer Is The Tip Of The Spear Of Your Sales Message

In most cases, a strong offer will succeed in spite of weak copy, but strong copy won't overcome a weak offer. The best laser-targeted traffic in the world can't save an ordinary 'good enough' offer. In other words, you can have the latest landing page building software, the most advanced sales funnel possible with contingency campaigns up the wazoo, the best Google Ads or Facebook ads guru running the most advanced traffic campaigns, heat mapping software installed on your website – but if you don't have an irresistible offer for your market, then *none of that matters.* It really is the offer that makes the heart beat and blood pump in your marketing.

A strong offer is not solely based on price. Don't think you must have the lowest price in order to have the strongest offer. Having an offer based on the lowest price can easily be copied by your competitors. And whoever wins that race to the bottom usually loses, or they always lose, right? It's usually the opposite with our clients because having a potent offer allows you to command higher fees.

Don't Use These Weak Offers

Even if they happen to be valid reasons why people should do business with you, the items listed below are *not* irresistible offers that motivate people to do business with you:

☒ Great customer service

☒ Outstanding quality

☒ Being innovative

☒ Having a great team

☒ Being responsive to your customers' needs

☒ Having a great reputation.

I have a saying:

'If the offer and the guarantee don't keep the founder up at night, then they're not strong enough'.

You need to create a response from your prospects like, 'How can they possibly offer this?' Or, 'How can they guarantee so much?' Or, 'Are these people out of their minds?' It must look outrageous. It must make the decision a no-brainer for your prospects.

A compelling offer is infinitely more powerful than a convincing argument

The idea of a compelling offer is to remove all friction for a prospect to buy from you. You want to reverse that risk and burden and make it an absolute no-brainer for your prospects to take you up on your offer. In the words of the late, great Claude Hopkins, *'Make your offer so great that only a lunatic would refuse to buy'.*

The Seven Parts Of Your Godfather Offer

A Godfather Offer is comprised of seven major components that make its brilliance come to life:

1. Rationale

Compelling offers begin with a clear and credible explanation of why you're making such an outrageously generous offer. Perhaps it's a 'Special Introductory Offer' and you're so confident that once the prospect experiences the truly amazing benefits your product or service provides, they'll be a raving fan of your company and a customer for life. Or maybe you have a more efficient business model than your competitors and this allows you to pass the savings onto your customer – exposing a 'hoax' or a 'con' positioning yourself as a concerned advocate, casting stones at a shared enemy and becoming your new customer's greatest champion.

Whatever your reasoning and rationale for the amazing, truly spectacular and almost unbelievable offer you're making, put it up in lights and make it abundantly clear to ensure your offer is believable.

2. Build Value

First things first: You want to build the value of your offer based on the usual everyday price – this can be what you normally charge or even what your competition is charging.

It's important to establish your regular price and make it seem like really good value. To make your regular price believable, specifics and forensic-like detail are crucial for proof.

Tell your prospect where your product has been offered or sold at full price or even how many thousands of people have paid the full price for the product or service. Show, don't tell: Where possible, it's very important to include screenshots of other websites and catalogues. This makes it even more believable to the everyday sceptic that this is indeed true and you aren't building superficial value or hype.

Then, illustrate in great detail (sell) why even at full price your product is an incredible deal. Show how your product or service is a mere pittance to what they will make or save, even at the regular price.

Then reveal your discount in a way that illustrates your role as your prospect's advocate and champion.

Quantify the monetary benefits the product will deliver and compare it with the almost insignificant price you're asking in return. Reduce it down to the ridiculous. Breaking the regular price down to a daily or weekly figure and compare it with something far more trivial that they spend more on without even thinking about the expense: A cup of coffee or protein smoothie that's just $1.33 per day, week, month; or cheaper than a cup of coffee to get [insert huge benefits].

3. Pricing

If the offer you're making is designed to turn complete strangers into paying clients and customers, the key is to offer a low-end price point that will get you maximum numbers of new customers, *plus* one or two higher price points to increase your average sale and return on investment. You want to lead with your most aggressive offer and then have two to three upsells after the initial purchase has been made. This makes the first sale as attractive and irresistible as possible and once the prospect has bought the first offer, the additional upsells are met with less friction than if you would have offered a higher price on the front end.

You can even lead with a *loss leader* – an introductory product or service that you're willing to sell or give away at a loss in order to build customer loyalty and future sales. For example, one of the most profitable smartphone game apps in the world is Candy Crush. You may even play it yourself! And guess what? It's a 'freemium' app, which means you download the basic game for free. You can even play the basic game for free as long as you want to. *You are never required to pay a penny.* But Activision Blizzard, who now owns the game, earns a reported $633,000 *per day* by selling in-game upgrades for more moves, more lives, and more levels. The game is designed to make users an offer they cannot refuse – and sure enough, they love it and keep spending to play it.

The key here is to avoid presenting prospects with too many choices on the front end, and leave that to the upsell process. Your chances of losing the initial sale increase with every extra option to purchase they're offered. Any additional time your prospect spends trying to decide which offer to go for kills the sale.

Now if you're generating leads, your offer might be a free consultation. If that's the case, you still need to attach a dollar amount to the consultation and you still need to sell hard to get people to take you up on your offer, even if it's free.

Your offer should be specific, so you can't just slap a 'free consultation' as your offer and think you're done, no, no, no. Offer a free 30, 45 or 60-minute phone consultation, analysis, strategy session or roadmap.

More on this in the 'Putting Together Your Landing Page' section of this chapter.

4. Payment Options

When your ideal price point – the level at which most of your customers will buy – is relatively high for prospects, consider breaking up the purchase into a payment plan of three or four payments.

You collect the credit card number with the order, then charge it for one-third or one-fourth of the total amount each month for three or four months.

By doing so, you effectively lower the perceived price point in your prospect's mind and this should increase response. Plus, 'today' money is always more crucial to a prospect's decision to buy than 'tomorrow's' money.

5. Premiums

These are the free gifts that prospects receive along with the product they're purchasing.

Premiums are not to be scoffed at. You might be rolling your eyes and thinking about late night infomercials that gush, 'But wait… there's more! You'll also get this free set of steak knives – *if* you order *right now!*'

The reason premiums are used is because *they work*. Having a hot premium can double or triple your sales. When you start paying attention to commercials on television and in the media, you'll realise the ones that really work, the ones advertising with real force and spending hundreds of millions of dollars – they mostly have premiums.

Why? Do you think they enjoy burning their money and eroding their margins? No! It's because they dramatically increase response.

A great example of the impact of having a hot premium is from *Sports Illustrated*. In the summer of 1986, Martin Shampaine, the magazine's marketing manager, found himself in the difficult situation where his last few promotions had bombed, meaning he wasn't persuading enough people to subscribe, which is basically the worst news any magazine can get. So, he needed something new, something fresh – an offer people couldn't resist.

It was then that the Football Phone premium was born.

Sports Illustrated ran television ads giving away the

football phone as a premium with a yearly subscription of the magazine. This premium went on to sell 1.6 million subscriptions for the once-hurting publication.

Premiums are a proven way to pull in more sales. And no, if you're a homebuilder it doesn't mean you should offer your new clients a football phone. Great premiums should be aligned and relevant to your business.

Here are some premium examples:

Identify theft insurance company: Free document shredder.

Homebuilding company: $5,000 furniture and appliances voucher.

Car detailing company: New floor mats.

Moving company: A 'get your bond back' small home repair tool kit or free end of lease cleaning service.

Divorce lawyer: Free $500 travel voucher (romantic getaway or get some space!)

6. Power Guarantee

The stronger your guarantee, the better. The role of the guarantee is to reverse the risk for the prospect and place it on you, the business, thus removing some of the friction before making the sale. Twelve-month guarantees tend to be the most common. However, it's much better to be very specific and if the guarantee is attached to the performance of what you're selling: 'If you follow the program and don't lose 10kg in your first 180 days, just let us know and we'll refund every cent you've paid'.

We'll be diving into the exact specifics of guarantees later in this section.

7. Scarcity

Offers without scarcity don't sell as well, but it needs to be genuine or you'll erode brand trust with your prospects. Think about it, if you don't need to take action now, when will you take it? Never.

Examples of scarcity include:

☑ Putting an expiration date on your offer.

☑ Countdown clocks.

☑ Only X left at this price.

☑ Buy before X to avoid a price hike.

☑ We only have so many hours in a day/employees to service you/products left in the warehouse.

Scarcity has been shown time and time again to

dramatically increase the pulling power of offers. The best marketers use it because it works. Injecting scarcity into your offer tells prospects they're being offered something unique – but they need to act fast!

Anticipate And Overcome Objections

After you've mapped out your offer, you now want to ask yourself what objections a sceptical prospect might have in taking you up on your offer.

Spend some time thinking about the objections your prospects would have and write them down below.

What are the main objections to the offer?

1.

2.

3.

How will you overcome these objections?

1.

2.

3.

Once you've completed this, it's time for the last step – to read your offer and ask yourself, 'What can I add to make this offer *even more* compelling?'

Once you've made your offer as irresistible as humanly possible, then make sure the copy is tightly written. Offer copy needs to be direct and to the point. There can be no confusion about what the prospect will receive in exchange for their money or time; when they'll receive it and why it will benefit them. That means you must edit your offer copy even more ruthlessly than normal, making sure everything is crystal clear.

I can't stress the importance of labouring over your offer. Once you know what your market wants and you package it all up in the most irresistible offer possible, everything else becomes a lot easier. And once you experience a taste of what a Godfather Offer brings to your bottom line, you'll never look at it the same way again.

A 'Power Guarantee' That Slaughters Your Competition And Leaves Them Screaming For Mercy

Here is a simple but devastatingly effective sales strategy that can help dramatically transform your business.

I'm now going to show you how to eradicate sales resistance and scepticism through having a **power guarantee.** This simple approach builds trust and goodwill, while getting you more customers than you know what to do with.

While just about everybody's heard of a guarantee, very few marketers and business owners know how to craft one that takes full, 100% advantage of its incredible selling power.

And that's precisely what the following content is all about.

I'm going to take you by the hand and show you how to take your ordinary guarantee and pump it up with steroids. You'll discover how to soothe even the most sceptical prospects and make your guarantee so compelling it cripples the competition and brings them to their knees, pleading for mercy.

WAIT A MINUTE! What in the world am I hearing? You say you don't already have a guarantee? Are you trying to tell me you thought all you had to do was tell your prospects how great you are and they would line up waiting to throw their money at you?

Well, unfortunately, that's not quite how it works.

So, before we get to work, let me address some of the biggest concerns around having a guarantee and what your inner pessimist might be thinking right now....

'I don't want to offer a guarantee...'

Listen: If you're not willing to guarantee your products and services in some way, shape or form, why should any of your prospects trust you?

Think about that for a moment. If you're not willing to

guarantee any element of the products and services you sell, why on Earth should anybody trust you with their hard-earned money?

How are you different from all the other companies they've done business with, only to be left with empty promises and disappointment?

You need to realise your prospect has been let down, misled, and downright lied to by other businesses. They're sceptical. And if you're not willing to offer a guarantee for your product or service, how can you possibly put those fears to bed?

Think about this – if you don't have a guarantee, you're literally placing all the risk of your prospect's purchase on them and no risk on you. What does that say about your business? If you're really planning on growing and scaling your business, it means the majority of the advertising you do is going to cold traffic – that is, people who don't know, like, or trust you. These are people who are just online. They've been doing their research. They've seen your Facebook ad, Instagram ad, or whatever it might be. Essentially, you're asking a complete stranger to part with their hard-earned money for a product or service they don't even know is going to solve their problem. Right? A powerful guarantee reverses that risk, and it reduces the friction for someone to buy.

You want to lead with the Godfather Strategy, which is to make them an offer that's so good they can't refuse. And then you want to back that up with the whole 'you can't lose' guarantee, and reverse all that risk. If you're confident with what you're selling, why wouldn't you make it as easy as possible for as many people to buy your products and services? To do otherwise just doesn't make any sense.

If you're still not quite on the same page, let me ask you this question: What would you do if the customer bought from you, and then, for one reason or another, they weren't satisfied with what they bought? How would you make it right?

Would you tell them, 'bad luck'?

Would you say, 'Look, you've bought it, it's your problem now'?

Or would you work with them to ensure they're happy, and add even more equity to your brand name by really helping them?

The answer should be obvious.

However, if it's not, let me bring something else to your attention. By law in most countries, if someone buys from your business, and something is defective or doesn't perform as advertised, or could be perceived as not being truthfully advertised, the consumer is entitled to compensation with either repair or replaced goods, or part of them; resupply or fixing a problem with services, or a part of them; or providing compensation to the consumer or end-user. In Australia, consumer protections are enforced by the Australian Competition and Consumer Commission, so you already have a guarantee. Whether you like it or not, it's built into everything that's sold in this country. So, if you've already got a guarantee, then why not advertise it? Use it to your advantage to reduce buyer friction and increase your selling power. A powerful guarantee can triple sales, and they're called upon less than 5% of the time. So, if you do the math, you can tell me whether or not you think that's a calculated play to use this front and centre of all of your marketing.

The Deeper Psychology of a Power Guarantee

In order to fully capitalise on the selling power of your guarantee, you must grasp the primal psychology behind it.

The primary thing to realise is this: In any given transaction between two parties, there will always be risk present. In most cases, one side will be asked to assume the burden of this risk, and more often than not, it's generally the buyer, and not the seller.

For your prospects, the biggest risk they have is believing your promise to them. In essence, you're asking them to have faith and believe that what you're telling them is true. That they should simply 'take your word for it' and that they'll experience the numerous benefits you're promising.

And who could blame them for being reluctant to trust you? In an age where so many false promises are made and scepticism is so rampant, prospects must be very careful about accepting anything you tell them. Unfortunately, in every market there are people out to make a quick buck by promising a diamond and delivering a hunk of cheap glass. Even if you have plenty of proof, testimonials, and other credibility elements to showcase, your guarantee is one of the most important credibility elements in your offer. You should go beyond thinking of it as a simple 'risk reversal', designed to push fence-sitting prospects over into taking action on your offer. Instead, think about your guarantee as a *proof element* to your overall offer – proof of how confident you are about delivering on every promise your offer makes.

The primary function of your guarantee is to make your prospect feel safe and secure that they'll get everything you've promised them or their money back.

And don't worry, I know what you're thinking: 'If my customers can try the product before they pay, and return it without owing a cent, surely they'll take advantage of me and I'll lose money hand over fist and go broke!' Know this, for every dishonest scammer who takes advantage of your liberal guarantee policy, you'll get five honest prospects to say 'yes' when they otherwise would have been too uneasy or sceptical to buy.

This has been proven time and time again in thousands of scientific split tests.

7 Steps To Creating A Power Guarantee

Ok, let's get busy: here's a step-by-step method for creating your power guarantee (or pumping up an existing one on steroids) and using it to supercharge your marketing efforts.

1. Study the competition

Do a Google search for other businesses in your industry and the word 'guarantee'. Then take it one step further and have someone call and ask them about their guarantee. Look outside of your industry or geography for solid guarantees. Write them down. Go deep in your search. What trends do you see? Do many companies in your industry offer guarantees? What type of guarantees did you find? Did you find any specific performance-related guarantees or were they the more common, lacklustre vanilla 'satisfaction guaranteed' type?

2. Laser in on your strengths

What area of your business is a strong point for you? Do you get results quickly? Do you have exceptional craftsmanship? Do you do very fast installations? Are you great at maintenance? Do your products or services produce consistently outstanding results? Do you save money or time for your customers? Always sell the thing you do better than your competition.

3. Be specific

Think about the specific results a customer wants, or the problem they're trying to solve when they buy your products or services.

Your guarantee should be specific, not some vague notion of 'satisfaction'. Satisfaction is too broad. Make a specific promise and tell your prospects they must experience the benefits you're promising – otherwise they don't owe you a red cent.

What good things happen when a client uses your products or services? Better sleep? More money? Lose weight? Reduced stress? Write down the answer in detail and then guarantee that outcome. Do not simply guarantee 'satisfaction'. **Guarantee in detail what that satisfaction will look like to your customer and make it measurable.**

4. Choose a payback

As unlikely as it is that you'll be making good on your guarantee (remember, fewer than 5% of customers will ever take you up on it), you want to create an attractive payback in case a customer is unsatisfied. Ideally, it won't cost you much but will have a high perceived value, and alleviate and remove the perceived risk around the purchase. Your guarantee should exceed customer expectations, be memorable, and wow them.

5. Test, measure, and refine

It's vitally important that you know how well your

guarantee is performing before you make it a core element of your offer. How? You can include it on some landing pages and not others, or different advertising channels such as Google, Facebook, YouTube, or Instagram. Then track the results and test, measure, and refine it until it's really power packed and pulling in sales.

Pinpoint how much sales have grown over the same period last year or the period before you had a guarantee. Be sure to test at least two combinations of your guarantee to find the one that pulls in the most sales. You might guarantee results for 30 days in one test and 90 days in another (longer guarantees generally work better). You might even use a ten-year or, better yet, a lifetime guarantee as an experiment!

6. Put it front and centre

Once you've tested, measured, and refined your guarantee and found a winner that's pulling its head off, put your guarantee in writing and place it front and centre of all your marketing and public relations. Put it on your website, landing pages, proposals, in your ads, your brochures – anywhere a customer will see it.

7. Give your guarantee a name

While this isn't mandatory, giving your guarantee a unique name can dramatise it and heighten its impact. Here are just a handful of examples to get your creative juices flowing:

- 100% Money-Back Guarantee

- My 100% Money-Back 'Triple-Protection' Guarantee

- Take it to the Bank!

- Better than Risk Free

- You Can't Lose

- Unconditional, Money-Back Guarantee

- Your Money-Back, No Questions Asked

- I Personally Guarantee

- No Way You Can Lose

- 30-Day Free Examination

- No-Questions, No-Quibbles, Money-Back Guarantee

- Iron-Clad Money-Back Guarantee

- 100% On-the-Spot Full Refund

- My 110% 'Call Me Crazy' GUARANTEE!

- Absolutely No Risk to You!

- 100% No-Hassle Refund!

- My 110%, No-Fuss, No-Questions, 'Take-It-or-Leave-It' PROMISE!

- No Pussyfooting Around and Get Every Cent Back GUARANTEE!

- Stronger than Steel No-Risk Money-Back Guarantee

Here Are Some Industry-Defining Guarantee Examples:

The Forever Guarantee: If at any time you are not completely satisfied with the performance of your Cutco Product, we will correct the problem or replace it.

The $1 Million Service Guarantee: LifeLock works to help stop identity theft before it happens by taking proactive steps to reduce your risk. But if you become a victim of identity theft while you are a LifeLock member because of some failure or defect in our service, contact us and we will act on your behalf to repair any damage. We will spend up to $1 million to hire lawyers, investigators, consultants, and whatever else it takes to restore your name and help you recover the direct losses from the identity theft.

Domino's Pizza: Your pizza will be delivered in 30 minutes… or it's FREE!

Costco: 100% satisfaction guaranteed. We guarantee your satisfaction on every product we sell with a full refund. We will refund your membership fee ($55) in full at any time if you are dissatisfied.

With the seven practical steps you now hold in your hands, every guarantee you write should suck in sales like never before. Each step in this process is easy to apply, especially if you use one of the many examples I've provided as a template and adapt it to your own product or service. A strong guarantee puts your prospect at ease and makes it easier for them to say 'Yes!'

Follow these steps and do them well... then craft an irresistible Godfather Offer and throw that on top... and you've got a money-multiplying formula for wealth in virtually any industry.

Now get to it!

Action Points

- You create a FEATURE LIST.

- You create a BENEFIT LIST.

- You reduce your OFFER to writing.

- You offer a POWER GUARANTEE.

Putting Together Your Landing Page

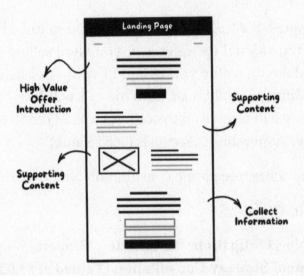

If you're a coach, consultant, freelancer, or run a professional services business and your goal is to generate leads, your Godfather Offer should be about making an offer for a free 30, 45, or 60 minute phone consultation, analysis, strategy session, or roadmap.

Why? If you're selling professional services, this typically involves you getting on the phone and speaking with people in order to convert a prospect into a paying client. Therefore, we want to make an offer to get as many of the people who raised their hand and identified themselves as being interested in what you're selling by downloading your HVCO to book in a call and speak to you.

This call must have a high perceived value, and it must

stand alone as something of value whether or not they choose to buy from you. You need to detail exactly what the prospect will get during the call and how it will help get them one step closer to their goal.

Just because it's free doesn't mean you don't need to sell it. You must detail the offer as if you were selling it for a price. Make the value you assign to your offer believable by detailing not only how long the call will last, but also what they will receive on the call, such as a Free 30-Minute Security Vulnerability Analysis ($685 Value).

Here are some free phone consultation offer examples:

Example #1:

Free No Obligation 45-minute 'Property Tycoon' Investment Strategy Consultation (Valued at $1,000)

During your call you'll discover…

- 5 most profitable property hot spots for your budget and ideal location.

- 7 insider tips on how to navigate the property tax world and uncover your hidden tax advantages.

- Which property markets give you the highest possible return on your investment.

- 3 financial traps which stop most Aussies going from one-time investors to property tycoons.

- How you can easily catapult your portfolio from 1 or 2 properties to 10 or more in just a few years.

Plus, we'll give you access to our exclusive Master Investor finance strategy which has helped people just like you go from everyday Aussies to wealthy property investors!

Example #2:

Claim Your Free Bulletproof Business Protection Consultation + 24-Point Business Security Checklist (Value $347)

Have our senior security specialist with over 20 years' experience, analyse your business's hotspots at risk for robbery. He'll then provide you with the exact system you need to keep your business safe and secure so you're not lying awake at night worrying about the safety of your business.

Here's what you'll get at your 100% free consultation:

- **A 360-degree vulnerability analysis where we identify the hidden areas through which burglars and gangs could attack your business.** Plus, we'll show you how to keep your weak spots protected and secure 24/7.

- **Tips and strategies that shield your property's 'blind spots' from vandalism, graffiti, and intruders.** (There have been 380,150 incidents in Melbourne this year alone – don't add your business to the list!)

- **Think if you've been robbed once, now you're safe? Wrong!** When thieves know a business is vulnerable, they'll come back, targeting it two, three, or even four times, costing the owners $10,000s in stolen goods, repairs, and lost work!

- **How to spot fake security system installers who are really criminals trying to rip you off** (These slimy thieves are nothing but con artists casing your business so they can swipe your goods!)

- **The easy and affordable way to beef up your security and make your premises feel like Fort Knox on lockdown.** And there's no need to break the bank to feel safe like the old days – we have top-quality systems for all budgets!

- **We'll show you the areas where shoplifters and two-faced employees can rip you off without you even knowing!** Catch these slimebags red-handed and put your hard-earned cash back in your pocket!

- **Our 24-point Security Checklist covers every vulnerable spot through which devious thieves can break into and destroy your business.** You'll also get solutions that safeguard your property, eliminate the threats, and protect your livelihood once and for all!

Notice the specificity and how they sell the call. Because if you don't sell it, you won't have any leads to sell. This conversation can close up to 80% or more of prospects, depending on your market and your own individual results.

You might be selling e-commerce products online. If that's the case, you can use the 17-step selling system below to go straight for the sale, skipping Phase 6 in the process, as this is both your landing page and selling mechanism in one.

Follow this process precisely and you will have more clients and customers than you know what to do with!

Sabri Suby's 17-Step Secret Selling System

Assembled into my exclusive Secret Selling System are the 17 fastest sales-producing secrets known to man! These powerful solutions can be used to sell just about anything to anybody, under almost any circumstances.

My 17-Step Secret Selling System can be used to create sales messages of any kind, whether it's for landing pages, sales videos, blog posts, webinars, or sales presentations.

It's every element you should include in any sales message. I have used my 17-Step Secret Selling System to generate over $400 million in sales for my clients and me. Follow this exact process and I'm confident it will help you smash your offers out of the park, every time.

Ready? Let's get started!

1. Call out to your audience

Address your audience at the start of your ads, at the top of your landing page or sales letter.

2. Demand their attention

Use a big promise headline, like the *National Enquirer* (Example: 'How to lose 10 Kgs in 6 Weeks Without Exercise Or Dieting…Guaranteed!')

3. Back up your big promise

After your big promise headline, back it up with a straightforward explanation in the subheadline.

4. Create irresistible intrigue

After you've crafted a headline that demands attention and a subheadline which positions your big promise, it's now time to dial up the intrigue with some bullet points. Write out 10 to 20 additional headlines and trim down to your best six. Each bullet should call out the difference pains, fears, hopes, and dreams of your target market and add an element of intrigue – such as, 'The Little-Known Secret to _____ that _____ Don't Want You to Know'.

5. Shine a floodlight on the problem

Identify the audience (who they are, how they feel) or tell a story about a problem, a struggle, or a challenge. Explain vividly how it feels to experience the specific problem your target market has. They should feel as if you're reading their mind and be left saying, 'Yeah, that's exactly how I feel'. Agitate the problem so they really feel pain and agony and become motivated to take action. Remember, people are much more motivated by moving away from pain than moving towards pleasure.

Talk about and describe in vivid detail what they've tried before to fix the problem and why it hasn't worked.

6. Provide the solution

Reveal a solution to their problem with your products

or services and then prove this solution is the best viable option that exists. Demonstrate clearly how it's different from all the other solutions they have tried which failed.

7. Show your credentials

Prove to them you can be trusted, establish your credibility, and demonstrate your expertise.

At this stage, your reader's scepticism is high and must be quietened. They're telling themselves, 'Sure he says he can fix my problem. That's what they all say. I've been told this a hundred times'. So, prove to them you can be trusted by showing them your credentials. For example:

- Results you've achieved.

- Successful case studies.

- Prestigious companies (or people) you've done business with.

- The number of customers you've served.

- Press mentions you've received (any and all).

- Important awards or recognitions.

Your reader must feel 'you've been there and done that' with great success and that they can expect the same.

8. Detail the benefits

People don't care about you or your product or service, they only care about what it will do for them. Features tell and benefits sell, so *talk only in benefits*. Use bullet points to call them out. Make a two-column list; in one column have all the features and in the second column have the corresponding benefit.

9. Social proof

You must build credibility and believability in your business and your offer. Use third-party validation to build authority, such as research statistics or quotes from credible or authoritative sources.

10. Make your godfather offer

In order to convert, your offer must be:

Clear and easy to understand: There should be no question as to what your audience is getting in return for their email/purchase/registration.

Value-based: Your offer copy should be focused on how it will fill a need or solve a problem.

Concise: Keeping it short and to the point will drive more conversions.

Persuasive: If there ever was a place to bust out your salesperson chops, your offer is it.

Irresistible: It must be such a good offer that it's a no-brainer for your prospect and even leaves them asking themselves, 'How can they possibly offer so much value?' Make it so compelling that only a lunatic would refuse!

11. Add bonuses

Add relevant bonuses or sweeteners to the offer. These

should be highly desirable but not essential to reaching the desired outcome – prospects simply need to want them.

12. Stack the value

Use the value stack to do just that... stack up the total value and benefits of everything in your offer. Tell them how much everything is worth then paint a vivid picture with benefit explanations to raise your offer's perceived value.

13. Reveal your price

Add prices together to calculate value, then reveal a price that's much cheaper. Explain why the price is what it is and why it's such great value. If your goal is lead generation and you're pitching a free consult, it's important that you put a dollar value on what the consult is worth. This is not to be confused with the price of your services; you can cover that on the call.

14. Inject scarcity

Offers without scarcity don't sell as well, but it needs to be genuine or you'll destroy your reputation. Think about it: If you don't need to take action now, when will you take it? Never.

Examples of scarcity include:

- Putting an expiration date on your offer
- Countdown clocks
- 'Doors are closing'
- 'Only X left at this price'
- 'Buy before X to avoid a price hike'

Scarcity has been shown time and time again to skyrocket conversion rates. The best marketers use it because it works.

15. Give a powerful guarantee

Remove, eliminate, reverse, and take out perceived risks. Longer guarantee = less returns. A guarantee transfers the risk from the buyer to the seller. And it shows the buyer that if the product doesn't deliver, they won't be at a loss of time or money, thus eliminating the pain of buying. Whether it's a no-risk money-back guarantee or a promise to not share their information, guarantees remove the risk associated with your offer.

16. Call to action (CTA)

The call to action is a command. Be specific and tell them exactly what to do. Keep it clear and direct – your audience shouldn't have to play 21 Questions to figure out what you want them to do. Ask them to do just one thing, because the more hoops you ask them to jump through, the more likely they'll be to say 'screw this' and leave.

17. Close with a P.S. that includes a warning and a reminder

Always include a closing point or P.S. It's the third most read element of your letter. Remind them of your irresistible Godfather Offer. Warn them against the consequence of what will happen if they don't buy. Include your call to action and remind them of the limited time or quantity.

Action Points

- Write down the *most irresistible and absolute best offer* you can come up with. Even if it scares you – then you know you have a great offer.

- Create an irresistible landing page, video sales letter, or whatever delivery mechanism will work best for you and your prospect, using my exclusive 17-Part Secret Selling System and example templates provided.

- Pitch the phone call and not the sale. While you ultimately want to convert your prospects into paying clients, in order for that to happen you'll need to speak with them. With that in mind, make your Godfather Offer centred around a free phone consultation, analysis, strategy session, or roadmap.

PHASE 5:

Traffic

Send Your Offers into the Endless Raging River of Online
Traffic to Reach Larger Numbers of Your Dream Buyers

Once you've got Phases 1, 2, 3, and 4 in place, you're now ready to put the machine in motion. You've done your research and identified your Dream Buyer, you have created your HVCO, an opt-in page, and presented your Godfather Offer on your landing page to get prospects signed up. Now it's time to look at what traffic channels are right for your business, and then craft the most irresistible click-worthy ads to pull prospects into your machine.

But before you do, it's essential you get your head around the critical importance of unit economics. These are the fundamental numbers your business growth hinges on. With this information, you can work out exactly how much you can spend to acquire a customer while still turning a healthy profit.

The Critical Importance Of Unit Economics

In order to determine the health of your business and whether you can scale and grow, you need to have a keen understanding of unit economics. Unit economics is simply defined as: 'The direct revenues and costs associated with a particular business action, expressed on a per-unit basis'. You may have also heard them referred to as 'key performance indicators'.

Here are some examples of unit economics that are crucial for you to understand:

Cost per lead (CPL): You can calculate your CPL by dividing the cost of your advertising by the number of leads received for a particular campaign or marketing activity.

Cost per acquisition (CPA): This is what it costs you in advertising to acquire a new customer. In any business, this is the most important metric to understand. It's the only way to understand if the marketing you're doing is profitable.

Lifetime value (LTV): This is the projected net profit that a customer will generate during his or her life as a customer of your business.

Why is knowing unit economics so important?

Put simply, if you have a firm grip on your unit economics, you'll know exactly how much a customer is worth to your business over their lifetime. In other words, no more guessing how much to spend on your marketing – you'll have precise control and confidence down to the cent.

Armed with this information, you can begin to aggressively market and grow your business as you understand fundamentally how profitable your customer acquisition strategy is, and you can scale it faster and more efficiently than your competitors who don't understand these metrics. They might try Google Ads, look at the CPC (cost per click) and think, *'Oh wow! This Google stuff is really expensive'*, and stop, when in reality it might actually be highly profitable for their business if they knew they were making ten times that cost from customers coming to their business through that channel.

What should my cost per acquisition (CPA) be?

How do you figure out what your CPA is? And what makes a good CPA? In other words, how much should you be spending to get a new client? The answer, of course, is that it varies; it all comes down to your average revenue per customer.

There are plenty of ways to determine your average revenue per customer, but a good starting place is to take your total revenue over a period (year or month) and divide this by the number of customers you had during the same period.

For example, if your total profit for the year is $500,000 and you had 1,000 customers, your average profit per customer is $500.

There are other formulas that take into account purchase frequency, lifetime value, and average order size, but honestly, the formula above is the easiest place to start.

Know how much you make from a customer, and you'll know how much you can spend to get one.

In the above example, you can spend up to $499 to acquire a customer and you'll still make a profit. Of course, you'd want to make more than $1 profit per customer. I'm just using this as an extreme example, but you get where I'm coming from.

Armed with this number, take a good hard look at your current marketing activity. It should be obvious which channels are creating profitable customers and which channels are costing you more than they're worth.

Now, if you find yourself saying, *'Google Ads is too competitive'* or *'Google Ads is too expensive'* or worse, *'I tried Google Ads and it doesn't work for my business'*, then this thinking is going to leave your business stuck in limbo while your competitors continue to take your market share and grab all the low-hanging fruit.

Google Ads is simply one part of the puzzle, and when you shift your mindset, upgrade your learning curve, and use some of the tools I'm sharing with you, it's going to help your business skyrocket in growth and in profits.

A business should never rely on one single source of traffic for new business. Unfortunately, the following scenario is all too common:

A business starts advertising on an online channel, whether that be SEO, Google Ads, or Facebook Ads. For this example, we'll use Google Ads. They start with a small budget of $1,000 per month. They start getting some traffic, leads are coming in and they are converting those leads into sales. Things are going great.

They hire more people to deal with the influx of new leads and sales, and even increase their ad spend to get even more business. The business owner is really happy they've found an advertising channel that works to scale their business.

Then suddenly, without warning, Google changes the landscape of their ad platform.

On a Friday in February 2016, Google did exactly this. Google decided to remove the sidebar ads on search results. After this day, businesses who relied solely on Google Ads to get traffic, leads, and sales were hurt... badly. Google literally wiped off 70% of its ad real estate, so competition for the top spots on the remaining 30% soared. And with this increase in competition CPCs (cost per click) skyrocketed.

If such a sudden shift occurs to their primary marketing channel, the business may find itself with far less traffic coming to their website but with many more staff to pay. So they have to let go of the employees that they hired when the business was growing, as they no longer have a channel that's bringing in the same volume of traffic, leads, and sales.

New Version   Old Version

Many businesses made this mistake and suffered catastrophically in early 2016. But not all, and certainly none of the businesses I was helping to grow at that time. Why? Simply because the most successful businesses build multiple flows of traffic to maintain their flow of leads.

This is how you do it:

Start with one channel (SEO, Google Ads, Facebook Ads,

Instagram Ads, YouTube, LinkedIn, etc.). It depends on your budget as to which one you should choose first. Once you establish an offer that converts profitably and you're making more than you're spending, get clear on your cost per lead (CPL) and cost per acquisition (CPA) of getting a new client on this channel.

Assuming your goal is to scale your business, keep adding as many channels as possible, stacking one on top of the other:

- SEO

- Google Ads

- Facebook Ads

- YouTube Ads

- Retargeting

Keep adding as many channels as you can to increase your sales

Keep at each channel until you gain momentum and receive a minimum of 50% ROI. Then roll these additional profits into experimenting on a new channel. Use this channel as a benchmark for your CPL and CPA when comparing the success of your new channels.

You might start with SEO, and after six months, once you start getting an acceptable ROI, roll these profits into Facebook Ads. Bolster these two channels and ensure they are running profitably before you start scaling (increasing) ad spend and think about adding a third channel.

Ideally, you should have at least three channels firing along profitably, which will enable you to allocate some of your profit to other channels. If something changes in one, like the case above where Google dramatically changed its advertising landscape and CPCs skyrocketed, your business won't be as negatively affected because you can shift your ad budget for Google Ads into another channel and shelter yourself from such changes while you figure out how to get Google Ads back up to its original volume.

However, keep in mind that while many businesses (including marketing agencies) often think they just need more traffic, in reality what you need is an offer that converts traffic profitably.

For a business, having the ability to turn advertising into a profit is the single greatest skill to ensure you won't ever go hungry.

As a real-life example take Raphael Bender, whose ad campaign for Breathe Education started with one traffic channel that doubled his business. Adding more channels helped him scale his business from $200,000 to $2 million, and now we're taking him global. Once he had an offer that converted complete strangers into high-value clients, he grew from using Google Ads to SEO to Facebook Ads and so on, step by step, stacking on more traffic channels.

Because we developed a proven funnel, where we knew that for every $1 in traffic we put in it, it spat out $5, $8, and $10, we no longer had a traffic problem. That's the power of getting this system right.

As I mentioned in the introduction, most people don't have a traffic problem, they have an offer problem. Traffic is out there. More traffic than you know what to do with. And accessing it is the key to aggressively marketing and growing your business, rather than just hoping for the best.

But there are different types of traffic. You need to make your offer extremely enticing if you want them to click. Understanding where they are in the buying cycle – and what channel is best to reach them – is critical if you want to tailor a message to fit.

Make sure your message matches the temperature of your audience!

In Phase 1, I introduced The Larger Market Formula and the fact there are three different types of prospects you can attract into your business.

Three Types Of Traffic

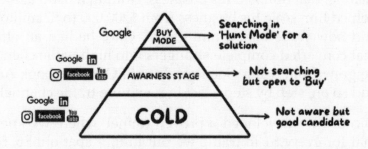

The first type, at the tip of the pyramid, is in buy mode. These guys are on Google, actively searching. They know they have a problem. They're looking for a solution in the products and services you provide. These prospects are generally best to reach through Google Ads or SEO, and they have a very high purchase intent. They could also be on your email list or following you on Facebook

The second group of prospects are in the awareness stage. They're not actively searching but they are aware they have a problem and they're open to buying. Perhaps they know they need a new car, but they're not scoping car yards on the weekends just yet. Or it might be someone who knows they need to lose weight but they're not yet in hunt mode looking for a personal trainer or a new diet program. These guys aren't searching, however they're certainly open to the prospect of buying. They're aware they have a problem, unlike the third type – the cold prospects.

A cold prospect isn't searching and doesn't even know they have a problem or a need. But they are still a good candidate for the products or services you sell. This represents the largest segment of your market, and of any market out there. They're the 60% of prospects sitting at the base of The Larger Market Formula pyramid.

So, let's say you offer a free consultation that's packed with value. How could it go wrong? Well, maybe your prospects are cold and not ready for that level of commitment just yet. Maybe it feels threatening to them. Maybe they don't want to speak to a salesperson.

If your message is not speaking to the temperature of your audience, it's never going to work. If your customers are cold, then offer a more cold-suitable call to action (CTA) such as a quiz, free guide, or competition. If your customers are piping hot, don't beat around the bush – take them straight to the shopping cart.

Think of it this way: If you went to a restaurant and ordered a medium-rare steak only to be served a steak so well done it might as well be a hockey puck, let's be real: you'd be sending that steak back.

On a steak, the temperature has to be right before serving. And the same thing is true for ads, offers, and landing pages. If you want to convert your visitors, you have to match the temperature of your audience.

Let's look at it this way.

Cold: Tinder Traffic

Tinder Traffic (as I like to call cold traffic) consists of people who have no idea who you are. Just like a Tinder profile, you're a complete stranger, and what they see on your ad or landing page will determine if they want to 'swipe right' and know more.

Warm: Second Date Traffic

Second Date Traffic (warm traffic) is – you guessed it – just like a second date. They've met you, they know you, but they're certainly not sold on you. They're trying you out to see if it's a fit, but one wrong move and you're history.

Hot: Netflix and Chill Traffic

Netflix and Chill Traffic (hot traffic) are the audience equivalent of a long-term relationship. They've worked with you in the past, they know all about you, and they'd spend all their time with you if they could.

Now, if you serve a Netflix and Chill message to Tinder Traffic, their reaction is going to be, 'I have no idea who you are, so…. Yeah, this is just too personal'. But if you serve a Tinder message to your Netflix and Chill audience, they're going to think, 'I'm offended – it's like they don't even know me!'

If you want to maximise conversions, you need to consider the temperature of your traffic and adjust your message to fit. Everything about your ad, offer, or landing page must be targeted to maximise the relationship you have with your traffic.

The plan is to take them from Tinder all the way past Second Date to Netflix and Chill. Here's how it's done.

How To Take Your Prospects From Tinder To 'Netflix And Chill'

Marketing is much like dating. There are a series of steps and events that must take place in order for a relationship to develop and get more serious.

Let's say the ultimate goal for dating is eventually to find a partner and get married. Generally speaking, the way you reach that end goal is by going through a series of steps and events. It might start with meeting someone at a party or bar, or through a friend. You might offer to buy that person a drink, share a conversation, or talk about star signs. If things go well and you hit it off, you exchange phone numbers.

After this, an 'offer' is generally made for a first date, perhaps dinner and drinks. Then a second date, perhaps a movie or a walk through an art gallery as you begin to get to know each other better.

You start dating. Things get more serious, you get engaged, and ultimately married. While there are certainly a lot more things that happen along the way, you get the picture. It's a process, with a varying level of commitment along the way to reach the desired outcome.

Business is much the same. However, most businesses are out there asking people to marry them on the first date, or even worse, at first sight!

What do I mean by this? Instead of capturing a lead by using a HVCO, building value through using the Magic Lantern Technique (we'll get to that in phase 6), educating your prospects, and only then asking the prospect to buy, most businesses are out there screaming at the prospects to buy straight out the gate.

Right from their advertising and ads they're screaming,

'We've got the best range and the best service… *Come and buy* our stuff'.

From experience working with thousands of businesses over the years, this is the biggest mistake I see them making. They're walking into bars and asking people to marry them.

This is the completely wrong approach.

Whether you're advertising on Google, Facebook, Instagram, or YouTube, the very first step in the process of taking disinterested wanderers and turning them into your most valuable dream clients is **getting eyeballs on your ads.**

So let's take a look at the primary function of each step in the funnel to turn complete strangers into high-paying clients.

You are here

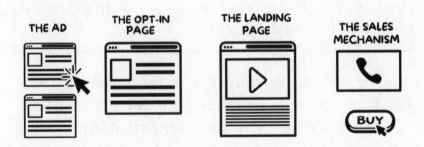

The job of the ad is to 'sell the click', its job isn't to sell your products or services. If your product or service can't ever be sold directly from the ad - why try?

The job of the opt-in page is to 'sell the opt-in', in other words, to get the prospect to opt-in and give their contact details in exchange for your HVCO, so you can follow up with them. This gets your prospects to raise their hand as being interested in what you're selling.

The job of the landing page is to 'sell the next step' if you're generating leads, this is where you want them to land. It's where you make your pitch to your prospects so they can book in a time to chat with you. Tip: make it all about them and not about you.

The job of the sales mechanism is to 'make a sale' whether you deliver your sales pitch over the phone, through a webinar or online via e-commerce. Everything leading up to this point has brought you here and now is your time to close the deal.

Starting with the very first step in the funnel – the ad – this might be on Google Ads, Facebook Ads, YouTube, Instagram, TV, or print advertising. It doesn't matter which channel or if it's online or offline, the premise is always the same.

The job of an ad is not to make a sale. It's one and only job is to *funnel prospects* off the medium they're on – Google, Facebook, etc. – by getting them to click.

Nothing else.

Before selecting which channel you're going to utilise, you need make sure the channel is right for the temperature of prospect you're targeting.

Let's start with Google Ads.

Prospects In Buy Mode

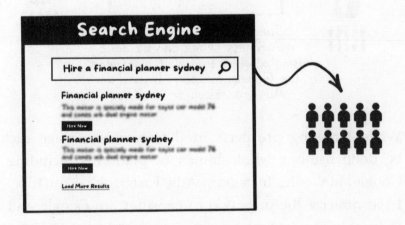

Targeting prospects in buy mode is best done using either Google Ads or SEO, and focusing on those super-high purchase-intent keywords and phrases. Here, you're specifically targeting the prospects who are fully aware they have a need and they're just searching for the right person to do business with.

Prospects In The Awareness Stage

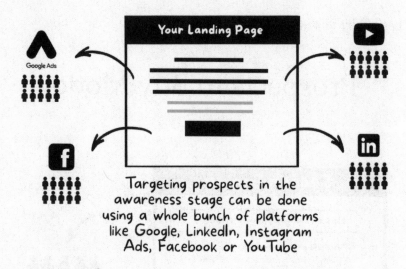

Targeting prospects in the awareness stage can be done using a whole bunch of platforms like Google, LinkedIn, Instagram Ads, Facebook or YouTube

While targeting prospects in the awareness stage can be done using a whole bunch of platforms including Google, LinkedIn, Instagram Ads, Facebook or YouTube, I recommend the only two to consider are Google and Facebook. They're the only grown-ups in the room. These guys have the duopoly on traffic online because they have the lion's share of the data. This means they can offer incredible targeting features that help you identify prospects who show buyer intent, matching all types of laser-targeted criteria from household income to purchase activity, and a ton of other unbelievable targeting options for your ads. When it comes to advertising online, this is where the opportunity is right now.

Recent stats say there are over 3.5 billion Google searches per day, and this number is increasing each year. People are getting more specific in their searches and these prospects have already sold themselves. They know they have a problem; they're motivated and out there looking for a solution.

Cold Prospects

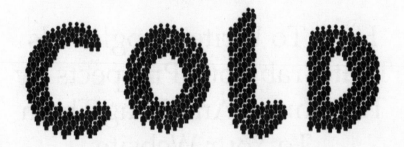

Cold prospects represent the largest segment of your market and can be accessed through Google, LinkedIn, Instagram Ads, Facebook, or YouTube. Targeting these prospects is ultimately where the biggest potential lies long term, but to warm them up you'll need a clever sales funnel with education-based content, such as what you'll learn in this book. Sounds complex, but trust me, it'll be worth the payoff when you start dominating your competition.

I know it's easy to start feeling overwhelmed at this point, so let's take a breather. Just imagine that Google and Facebook are raging rivers, full of your best kind of prospects. Your sole purpose is to get the attention of these prospects as they're racing past in that stream. When you break it down to those fundamentals, it's very simple. And though it can be tricky keeping on top of the interface changes on these platforms, the fundamentals never change because they're based in human psychology and the primal desires, fears, hopes, wishes, and dreams that drive us all.

We'll look at some proven ad formulas that tap into those desires in just a moment.

How To Write Google Ads That Grab Your Prospects By The Throat And Drag Them To Your Website

First, let's look at some stats. When you're running Google Ads, 2% of the advertisers get 50% of the traffic. So what really makes the difference? Well, I always see people using Google Ads to sell their products or services straight out the gate. They're using an ad to try to convince you they're the ones you should be doing business with. And that's ridiculous, because you can never, ever sell somebody from your ad. When was the last time you saw a Google ad and picked up and bought something without even clicking on the ad and checking out that website?

So if you can't possibly sell somebody directly from the

ad, why try doing it in the first place? It's just setting you up for a fail. And it comes down to this – your ad has one job, and it's not to try to sell something, it's to sell the click.

The job of an ad is not to sell the product; it's to sell the click.

Your ad has one purpose – to get people to click. Your ads should demand attention and compel readers to click, not buy. Imagine the advertising channel you're employing as a raging river full of prospects and your sole purpose is to get the attention of your dream buyer as they race past.

So that begs the question – how do you get their attention and what drives a click?

The answer is primal desire that can be provoked in a number of ways:

- CURIOSITY & INTRIGUE

- SHOCK

- DIRECT BENEFIT

- IMPLIED BENEFIT

- FEAR

- VANITY

- SELF-INTEREST (Better, Richer, Stronger, Faster, Healthier, Happier, Sexier, Fitter, Smarter)

To illustrate this, I conducted a quick Google search for 'divorce lawyers' and these were the ads I was presented with:

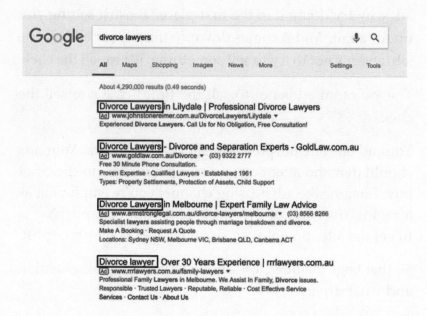

First up, all these ads look the same and all start with the words 'Divorce Lawyers'. None of them stand out and demand attention.

Next up, what are these ads trying to do? Sell me! Right there in the ad copy they are trying to convince me that they're the ones to help me and I should choose them. They're asking me to marry them on the first date.

'Specialist lawyers assisting people through marriage breakdown and divorce issues', 'Make a booking', 'Request a quote', 'Responsible' 'Trusted lawyers', 'Cost effective service' …

They're missing all the other steps in the process that come before this one and going straight for the marriage proposal. Why? Are they lazy? Do they simply not know any better? Whatever the reason, we're going to stop this madness right here, right now.

This is the right way to approach it. We must '*sell the click*'.

We do this by first assessing the environment in which our ad will compete for attention. We already know all the ads start with 'Divorce Lawyer', so we must do something different.

We also know that all the ads are screaming for a marriage proposal on the first date.

Let's get to work.

After a little research (using the Halo Strategy) to get the creative juices flowing, I came up with the following ad.

A Top Divorce Lawyers | Secret Checklist Finally Revealed
[Ad] www.exampledomain.com/Free_Report ▾
4 ★★★★★ advertiser rating
22 Tipoffs Your Husband May Be Cheating On You. Free Report Reveals All, Download Now!
Free PDF Report · 100,000 Downloads · Usually $69 Now FREE! · Ends Soon, Act Now!

Not a bad effort, I say. This is a simple ad I whipped up which 1) Sells the click by dialling up the intrigue with 'Secret checklist finally revealed'. Everybody wants to know secrets, and I've partnered this with 'Top Divorce Lawyer' to define what the checklist is going to be all about.

I then tease what's on the opt-in page and the reward for them to click, with: '22 Tipoffs Your Husband May Be Cheating On You – Free Report Reveals All'.

Nothing about this ad is selling anything. No one is ever

going to buy off the ad, so why try to sell them? Instead, offer something that's so irresistible, something that has so much intrigue that people can't help but click.

I then go on to build the social proof '100,000 Downloads' and add urgency 'Ends Soon, Act Now!' Now let's see how this ad shapes up in the environment where it has to compete for attention.

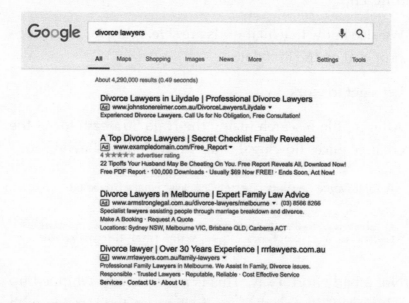

Which ad would you likely click on? Which one stands out? Which one is the least threatening? And which one has intrigue oozing out of it?

This is just one simple example. Opportunities exist like this in all markets. This one strategic shift can make you stand out head and shoulders above the competition and funnel the lion's share of prospects into your business.

There are a bunch of different winning ad types listed

below. Read them, think about why they work, and which approach would work for your market. There's no need to reinvent the wheel. Simply model what's already working and apply it to your own business.

Click-Worthy Google Ad Types And Examples

Ad Type: If they can, you can too

Fat Dad's 6-Pack In A Month - 6packdad.com
Ad www.6packdad.com/get-ripped
4.5 ★★★★☆ rating for 6packdad.com
Overweight 43-Year Old Reveals Lazy Way To 'Dissolve' Stomach Fat In Four Weeks.

Ad Type: Irresistible intrigue

What Abott Told Packer - buygold.com.au
Ad www.buygold.com.au/
4.5 ★★★★★ rating for buygold.com.au
The 10pm Phone Call That Will Change How You Invest In Gold in 2017.

Ad Type: Prediction-based

SEO Set To Die In 2019? | "I Suggest You Read This"
Ad www.kingkong.com.au/Free-PDF/Report ▾
4 ★★★★★ advertiser rating
Breaking: Brand New SEO Report Reveals All. Don't Invest a Cent Into SEO Before Reading This!
SEO Lies Exposed! · 3 Questions To Ask SEO's · SEO Agency Lying To You? · 8 Traffic Soaring Secrets

Ad Type: Fear mongering

Fish Oil Bad For You? - krilloil.com.au
Ad www.krilloil.com.au/Fish-Oil-vs-Krill-Oil
4.5 ★★★★★ rating for krilloil.com.au
New Research Shows Link Between Fish Oil And Premature Ageing. Read This Brand New Report Now!

Ad Type: Breaking news

Breaking News: Tesla Sells 325,000 Cars In 7 Days -
Ad http://www.etoro.com.au/Buy-Tesla-Stocks-Here
4.5 ★★★★★ rating for
Tesla Stocks Soar After Raking In $11 Billion Dollars In Pre Orders. What Did Elon Musk Do The Day After? Find Out Here:

Ad Type: Myth buster

5 Foods You Must Not Eat: - beyonddiet.com.au
Ad www.beyonddiet.com.au/5-Foods
4.5 ★★★★★ rating for beyonddiet.com.au
Cut Down A Bit Of Stomach Fat Every Day By Never Eating These 5 Foods.

Ad Type: Freebie / Discount

Pure Merino Wool Cardigan 40% Off -
Ad http://www.hedrena.com.au/7-Day-Sale
4.5 ★★★★★ rating for
1 Week Only Offer: Once You Wear Merino Wool You'll Never Go Back! Treat Yourself To The Very Best Here.

Ad Type: Testimonial

"My Sales Tripled In The First 90 Days" - InsideSalesTraining.com.au
Ad www.InsideSalesTraining.com.au/Double_Sales
4.5 ★★★★★ rating for InsideSalesTraining.com.au
Battle-Tested Sales Training Program That Guarantees To Increase Sales! Learn More Here.

*Please note: these are not real ads and are just being used for illustrative purposes.

More Click-Worthy Ad Examples (Google Ads)

Warning: Don't Get Ripped Off | Get Your Free Sample Service
[Ad] www.exampledomain.com.au/Free_Samples ▾
4 ★★★★★ advertiser rating
Bring Your Old Concrete Back To Life. Free Consultation & Service. Call Today!
100% Obligation Free Quote · Hidden Costs Exposed! · Free Samples Express Post!

Franchise Is Not The Way To Go | Become Your Own Boss [Free PDF]
[Ad] www.exampledomain.com.au/12_Fatal/Mistakes ▾
4 ★★★★★ advertiser rating
Download Our Free Ebook & Learn How To Avoid The 12 Fatal Mistakes Startups Make
Free PDF Report · How To Become Your Own Boss · Usually $97 Today Only Free!

Shocking Insider SEO Secrets | "They Don't Want You To Know"
[Ad] www.kingkong.com.au/SEO_Secrets/Revealed ▾
4 ★★★★★ advertiser rating
Make Sure You Read This Shocking Free Report Before Investing A Cent In SEO.
SEO Lies Exposed! · 3 Questions To Ask SEO's · SEO Agency Lying To You? · 8 Traffic Soaring Secrets

Caught Your Wife Cheating? | "I suggest you read this."
[Ad] www.marriagemax.com/7_Secrets_Free ▾
4 ★★★★★ advertiser rating
Free Report: 7 Secrets to Save Your Marriage. This works. As seen on Fox News.
Rated "A" by BBB · Over 90% Success Rate · Shopper Approved 5 Stars · Ranked #1 by the AMAA

Banned Seduction Technique Revealed - thepickupninja.com.au
[Ad] www.thepickupninja.com.au/
4.5 ★★★★★ rating for thepickupninja.com.au
The Most Sought After Seduction System In The World Revealed. How To Make Any Woman
Wildly Attracted To You!

*Please note: these are not all real ads and are just being used for illustrative purposes.

Now, one thing I want to highlight is that writing the perfect headline for your ad is a process. Don't try and nail the killer headline for your pay per click or Google Ads campaign the first time around. In my experience, it takes a minimum of 20 attempts to get the best headline. Some of the best headlines are like the Franken-headlines, where you see that one ad is working really well, and then another ad is performing somewhat well, and you mishmash all the elements and keep tweaking it and running different variations to find the killer ad that just crushes it in your space.

You need to think about what your target audience really wants. And I know you might be thinking, 'Well, Sabri's copy is a bit outrageous', but the thing is, average copy just wastes money. You need to be provocative. You need to shock people. You need to say the opposite of what your competition is saying. If you want to cut through the noise, and enter into a market and own that category, then you need to do something different to get attention.

My Google Ads Checklist

These are the nine key questions you should be asking yourself when it comes to Google Ads or PPC campaigns:

- Am I getting more money back than I'm putting in?

- Do my keywords match search terms my market is using?

- Are my conversions increasing every month?

- Is my cost per conversion decreasing?

- Are my visitor's needs aligned with what I'm offering?

- Does my copy demand attention and sell the click?

- Is my PPC strategy geared for sales?

- Is my tracking in place so I can determine which keywords are generating sales?

- Is my focus on EPC (earnings per click) and sales volumes?

Look at the amount of sales your ads are generating and check you're earning the most amount of money per click that you can.

Let's drill down into this one so it's super clear. If you're spending $1,000 on Google Ads per month, and you're paying $2 per click, and from those ads you're selling $3,000 worth of consultancy services, you're earning three dollars for every one dollar you put into that campaign. In fact, it may be a lot higher because $3,000 per month might be a retainer, and the average client may be with you for a 6- or 12-month contract. So you might find the average client is ultimately worth $24,000, and you're spending $1,000 (or less) to acquire a client who provides $24,000 in revenues over the lifetime value of that client. Looking at it this way, you're putting one dollar into your advertising, and your earnings per click are essentially $12. Meaning that, when you're running Google Ads, if you can get clicks for anything less than $12, you're making money straight out the gate.

That brings me to sales volume. One thing I see rampant online is consultants raving about getting an incredible return on their ad spend. A return on investment is obviously the most important metric to look at. However, there's no point in spending $100 per month and getting a 12,000% return on investment because it's such a small scale. So while you want to look at earnings per click, you also need to look at *sales volume*.

Naturally, as you start to spend more, your ROI may go down a little bit. That's one of the casualties of scaling up a campaign. But keep looking at that top line revenue and what those earnings per click look like, and focus on growing the revenue for your business, because that's the life blood. That's the oxygen. There's no point spending $100 on Google Ads a month and making $1,200. Rather you should spend $1,000 and make $6,000 back. While the ROI will be lower, your overall sales and bottom line profit will be much higher.

Now let's take a look at a platform that's getting bigger and more important every year, and how we can engage their users on a level that matches what they're already interested in. We're going to cast our net for cold prospects, and the only way to catch them is to speak their language and offer something they can't resist.

How To Write Facebook Ads That Force Buyers To Read Every Word Of Your Ads

Up until a few years ago, Google had the monopoly on traffic. However, there's been a dark knight rising, and that is Facebook. As this book goes to print, there are over 2.2 billion monthly active Facebook users world-wide.

What's particularly interesting is that 1.74 billion of those monthly active Facebook users are coming from mobile. This means that 94% of Facebook's monthly active audience are accessing the app through their mobile device. We know that whoever has the eyeballs is the one leading the industry. And Facebook certainly has the lion's share of eyeballs. It's not hard to see that when you look around, people are glued to this thing. Right?

There's pretty much no-one you can't reach through Facebook these days. Everybody is on this thing and it's only going to get worse – or better for us as marketers and business owners! While you want to make sure you don't personally fall prey to this kind of vicious time-sucking vampire, it's an incredibly powerful platform for marketers. There's such rich data and laser-targeted criteria for reaching your hardest to reach, best prospects and dream buyers, and you can access them in a matter of seconds.

We've looked at the three types of prospects you can attract into your business. Google is fantastic for reaching those in hunt mode, but that's really a small subset of the market. Remember, it's those prospects in the awareness stage and the cold prospects who are the largest opportunity for scale in your market. And with Facebook, you can laser in on those who are good candidates for your services even though they may not even know it yet.

So let's look at how people are engaging on this platform. What's the content they're really hungry for? What is it they're clicking on the most? Where do their interests lie and what are the most shared pieces in this space?

BuzzSumo is a powerful online research tool that shows us the kind of content that gets shared the most. On Facebook in 2017, BuzzSumo shows us that breaking news articles and exclusives made up the largest and most popular category in terms of shares and engagement.

This is what I want to get you thinking about as business owner or marketer when positioning your services on this platform. Because that's a hook and an angle you can really go for.

True, these categories are competing with hip-hop video clips and animal videos, which get shared a lot too. But these aren't going to be things you can leverage to get attention. It's content that reports some sort of findings, news, or research that does incredibly well on Facebook and can be applied to all businesses.

So instead of trying to swim against the raging river that is people's attention, remember the advice of Eugene Schwartz, one of the greatest advertising minds to ever live. He said, 'This is the copywriter's task, not to create mass desire, but to channel and direct it'. In this instance, we're talking about channelling people's desire to engage with *content that looks like news.*

Remember, your ad has one job and that's to get people to click. In order to do that it should look like breaking news or an exclusive article, because we know that will compel people to click on your ad, read it, and engage.

The ad is the tip of the spear, and it's not to be confused with trying to do the job of any of the other steps in your funnel. We're not trying to get people's contact details. We're not trying to get people to buy services or call directly off the ad. We're not even trying to get the viewer to know right off the bat who we are or what we're selling! That will come quickly – but it's not the first thing we present to them.

Let's not swim against that raging river of attention. Instead, let's just swim along with it and channel that desire to engage in that kind of content.

We've discussed what drives a click, and that's curiosity, intrigue, shock, or direct benefit that a person stands to get from clicking on the ad. That's the big promise we're going to offer in our ads.

So, to summarise, what we're looking at is using these primal desires and combining them with the breaking news hook, and that is the winning formula.

Remember, this isn't some kind of theory. I haven't just looked at this and thought, 'oh that's cool, let me look at what the most shared content is' and then sat down in a dark room and dreamed up an esoteric theory about how the world works. No. I've spent millions upon millions of dollars inside Facebook on their ad platform in Ad Spend. This is coming from inside the trenches, on the front lines, and testing it with my own money, to see what's working and what's not.

This is just an example of one of the ads I run that have generated millions of dollars. As you can see, it looks like a news piece: 'How I Went from $0 Cold Calling from a Rented Bedroom to $833,000 Per Month in Four Years'. There's nothing crazy and I'm not trying to sell anything. It looks like a feature you might find in Forbes or Inc Magazine. There's just a picture of me standing in front of a desk and that's about it. So, let's get to work on this.

Ad Copy Tips

You don't need to reinvent the wheel or try to be a world

-class copywriter. I'm giving you a model and a proven system that I already know works. You can just swipe it and deploy it in your own business, and watch those leads start coming in.

Follow the attention. Where are all the eyeballs right now? What content are people actually paying to read and engage with?

AARP Magazine is the number one selling magazine in the world by a country mile. 23,428,878 people read *AARP Magazine* every two weeks, which is almost 50 million people per month. You've seen it at the checkout counters at supermarkets, where there's a million and one things going on.

The writers at *AARP* know they have three seconds to grab that prospect by the jugular, get the attention of a busy parent at the supermarket checkout aisle when their kids are screaming at them and pulling on their pants and saying, 'Hey can I have this? Can I have that?' While the store clerk is talking to them, and the store is full of people, and there's people behind them, and trollies at their back, and there's a whole lot of things going on right now. These AARP guys have three seconds to grab that person with all this chaos taking place, with copy that's compelling enough to get them to pick it up, throw it on that checkout, and go ahead and buy it. That is no easy task.

How do they do that? Well, with killer headlines, and bullet copy, and fascination copy that's just burning with intrigue. 'Six Bad Habits That Are Really Healthy'. What are they and why are there six? What are those six things? I really want to know!

Another one, 'Oh No, My Aching Back. Five Causes of Pain That Will Surprise You'. If you have back pain, which a lot of people do, what are the five causes? They're going to be surprising to me, so I can't already know them. Again, they're luring me in. It's nothing too crazy, but it is intriguing. Is it a heart attack? Read this and be sure!

All they want you to do is pick up that magazine. They've got that bait on their hook and they're reeling you in. Here's one that I love: 'Live to 100, We Found the Secret Formula in a Remote Village'. Naturally, you want to know what that is, we all want to live longer, right? And there's a secret formula that was found in a remote village…

This isn't some cutesy copy they think might work well. This is something that's working to get 50 million people reading their magazines every month. I realise these are examples from a mass-market magazine, but this is where you'll find the highest paid copywriters. This is where you look to see what's getting people – *millions* of people – to buy content. We already know this interest translates to the online environment with news articles and breaking news getting the most shares and engagement. We simply want to model what's already working out there in the market.

Another great way to find popular content types is to go to BuzzSumo and type in the topic you're interested in. You might be a consultant helping financial planners generate leads using social media. Look at what's been the most shared content in that category, or that keyword you're focusing on. For example, looking at the keyword 'financial planner' I see that 'The Best Piece of Money Advice in Your 30s from a Financial Planner' had 3,700 shares, and it's the second most shared content for financial planners.

Or this one: 'After 10 Years as a Financial Planner I've Realized Almost Everyone Gets the Same Thing Wrong About Money'. Naturally, I want to know what that is. What is that thing? It's from a financial planner that's been doing this for 10 years, and I really want to know what that is.

You are beginning to see what's going on here. What's going to grab that busy person scrolling through Facebook by the scruff of their neck and pull them into your ads? It is an incredibly busy world out there. That's why breaking or shocking news articles are the kinds of things that stop people in their tracks and demands their attention.

Here's one of my ads that appears as news: 'Digital Marketing Expert Breaks His Silence. You'll Never Understand Just How Wrong Advertising Agencies Have It, Until You Read This Shocking Expose By Australia's Top Digital Marketing Mogul and Agency Owner of Australia's Fastest Growing Digital Marketing Agency'.

It looks like news, and it's not misleading because it is news. These are all real things I'm talking about here! I'm lifting the hood on all these things that advertising agencies don't typically want you to know.

King Kong Co.
Written by Hannah Douglas [?] · February 15 · 🌐

Attention Facebook™ Marketers

We have spent millions on Facebook™ ads over the last 12 months, running thousands of scientific split-tests in over 126 niche markets including B2B.

In doing so, we've generated over $200 million in sales for us and our clients.

Over this time period, we've documented the most remarkable secrets for boosting Facebook™ Ad performance to an astonishing degree and have included these trade-secrets in this just-released free report.

Inside you'll discover secret Facebook™ targeting methods that unlock "hidden" audiences and 'hyper active buyers' in 30 days or less.

Save yourself the time, pain and headaches of "learning" how to use Facebook™ ads effectively.

This report is yours 100% free, just enter your details and hit the "download" button in the box below, and these sales-exploding tips will be sent straight to your inbox.

Every second wasted without this crucial information is another dollar lost to your competitors.

BREAKING NEWS

SECRET FACEBOOK AD TARGETING REVEALED

HEADLINES: FACEBOOK NOW HAS 17 MILLION AUSTRALIAN USERS

Secret Facebook™ Targeting Methods Exposed

Secret Facebook™ Targeting Methods That Unlock "Hidden" Audiences & 'Hyper Active Buyers' In 30 Days Or Less.

KINGKONG.COM.AU   Download

Here's another ad that's going for the same breaking news angle. This one's for Secret Facebook Ad Targeting Revealed. We've got a picture of Mark Zuckerberg. It appears to look like news, and on the back of this you click it, and it takes you to our High-Value-Content Offer. However, what you can see here in the ad is that it's just staying true to exactly the job of that ad, which is to get clicked. I'm not trying to get people to opt in or to do anything right now. All I want them to do is click this ad. I'm just channelling their desire to know what the news is and bringing them through to the next stage in that simple four-step funnel.

Let's look at another example. It's for an institute that teaches people to become Pilates instructors. Let's look at some of the elements of the ad.

First of all, the thing that gets your attention is this image of people doing Pilates on a mat. Then there's a massive logo and Pilates Mat Cost R6600 Fit Pro, so you see immediately this is an ad. Then there's a date and all the ad copy. They're asking us to email them for more information right on the ad. They're already showing me that their intention is to sell something.

This is definitely the wrong way to do it. This doesn't look like news, nor does it have any components that tap into a desire. Let's have a look at a better way.

Here's what we did for a client. This looks like a news article: 'Find out how everyday Aussies are breaking the shackles of their 9-to-5 desk jobs, and trading in their corporate attire for comfy activewear, and earning a lucrative paycheck doing so…' It's very newsy. It's intriguing – so what are all these Aussies doing? There's an article here and the image looks like one that would be shared on a news website.

The headline grabs you with 'Find out' and 'breaking the shackles of 9-to-5', because who doesn't want to know how to do that? Next, 'This shocking new report reveals how thousands of everyday Australians are quitting their jobs and flocking to become highly paid Pilates instructors'. Again, you can see that it looks like an article. There are no prices, no dates, no mention of the business name or anything like that.

Here's another example. How to secure your first profitable investment property in just 60-days. Breaking news, attention first-time property investors. Again, it looks like a news article. There are a lot of things going on here and it really doesn't look like we're trying to sell property investment. We're just trying to get people to click into the contents.

This is for a weight-loss person. 'Breaking news, exactly how I lost 77kgs, and how you can too'. A picture of the guy eating ice cream who's saying he's lost 77kgs. Wow. What is this? Did you diet? This makes me want to get involved and click through.

Or this is another one, from direct response marketing giant Stansberry Research. Again, it looks like a news article or an opinion piece. 'Here's how millennials will get back at America's baby boomers. Check out this radical plan backed by several Ivy League economists'. Then there are pictures of some homeless people. 'Expert says this will be a national nightmare. The next big bankruptcy in America will be unlike anything we've seen in more than 50 years'. The whole ad is geared at getting me to click and read more about what's going on. That's going to take them to a content piece, and there'll be an offer on the backend. These guys are seasoned marketers, they know what they're doing.

Another one here by The Motley Fool Australia. 'Japanese Billionaire's Prediction Will Give You Goosebumps'. All the copy is geared around intrigue.

Anatomy Of A High-Converting Facebook Ad

Now let's look at the anatomy of a Facebook ad so that when you're writing yours you know the different elements.

The Intro Text

This is the very first thing the scroller will see. This is why you go straight in with the news angle or call out your audience at the very top, whether it's 'Attention business owners', or 'Attention mothers over the age of 25', or whatever it might be.

Test different lengths of copy in here. We do very long form copy, and then we do short-form copy. In most instances longer-form copy will do the best job but it's good to test everything.

The Ad Image

The ad image is a really important element and it's where I see most people getting it wrong. They're using glossy images with buttons to try to get attention. But the thing is, Facebook is a *native advertising platform*, meaning that advertising should look like normal content being shared. People tune out things that look like adverts. Your ad images shouldn't look like an ad.

In our Pilates example, there's a shot of people on Pilates machinery, yet there's nothing that shows it's an ad straight from the get-go.

You should remember that *Facebook doesn't like ad images with text*. In fact, until recently, Facebook advertisers were allowed to cover their ad images with no more than 20% text. This rule has since been relaxed, but Facebook is right: Ad images with no text – which look more like news or general-interest images – get a much better response than images containing text.

The Link Headline

The next thing, which is arguably one of the most important elements after the image, is the link headline. This is essentially the headline of the ad. Model the structure of your headline on AARP Magazine, or the National Enquirer, or news headlines. Or go to Google News and look at their headlines and trending news articles. Buzzsumo studied 100 million Facebook post headlines between 1st March and 10 May 2017. They analysed the number of words in article headlines and plotted this number against the average number of Facebook engagements for all headlines in their sample. The results are shown on the chart below.

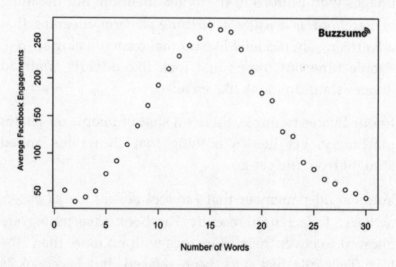

Number of Headline Words And Average Facebook Engagements

You can see that 12 to 18 words are the optimum number for high-performing Facebook ad headlines.

Not surprisingly, the number of characters has a similar

relationship to average Facebook engagements as the number of words. Based on research, 80 to 95 characters appears optimal.

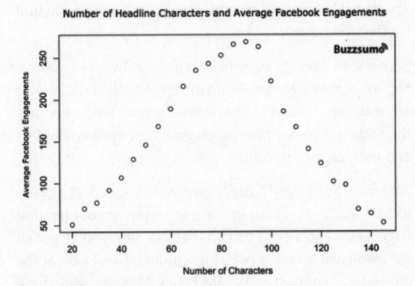

Number of Headline Characters and Average Facebook Engagements

The Link Description

The content below the headline, the link description, fleshes out your headline and gives readers a little bit more detail around what's going to be behind that click.

The Call to Action Button

There are a number of different alternatives you can use including 'Enquire now', 'Learn more', or 'Download', for example. We've found that 'Learn more' is the least threatening and converts best at the moment. So that's where I recommend you start. Everything's up for split testing. However, 'Learn more' is a safe bet.

The Display URL

The display URL is the web address of the page to which the prospect is going to be sent.

The social buttons, of course, show people engaging and sharing the content.

Remember, average copy wastes money. Don't be vanilla, be provocative. Do something different. Stand out. Look at what all the competitors are doing in your space, because their ads will be popping up on your newsfeed no doubt – and then do the opposite.

And most importantly, don't oversell in your ad. That's not its job. That's what your opt-in page is for, or your landing page. Once you've put that ad together, and you've got all the elements, just step back for a moment and look at the ad, and ask yourself... 'Would I click it? Is this something that would really intrigue me?'

Facebook Ads Checklist

- Does my copy look like news and demand attention?

- Are my Facebook ads selling the click?

- Is my tracking in place so I can determine which audiences and ads are generating sales?

- Is my focus on earnings per click (EPC) and sales volume?

- Is more money coming back to me than I'm putting into Facebook ads?

- Is my copy the perfect bait for my dream buyer?

- Are my conversions increasing?

- Is my cost per conversion decreasing?

PHASE 6:

The Magic Lantern Technique

The Single Most Powerful Strategy for Turning Complete Strangers into High-Paying Dream Clients Like Clockwork

Ok, that's enough theory. Let's show you how to put this all into action.

You start with a traffic source. It could be Facebook, Google Ads, Instagram, or even YouTube. You buy traffic from these channels at around $2 a click or less, and send them to an opt-in page. This is a webpage where a customer gives you their details – email, phone number, whatever – in exchange for something valuable. Your High Value Content Offer might be a piece of information, an ebook, or something else.

Once they've opted-in, they become a prospect, and you can market to them, virtually for free, using email. We find a combination of email with video generally works best.

They download your HVCO and then get redirected to a thank-you page, which is a landing page that presents your Godfather Offer to them. This page could be straight text, video, or a combination of both that presents your irresistible Godfather Offer.

Once the prospect clicks the button on this page to take up your offer, they are taken to a survey page where you can secure more details and arrange a call, on which you'd aim to make a sale immediately.

That takes care of the 3% who are in buying mode and eager to sail through your funnel to the purchase. But what about the other 97%? They enter your funnel, but because they're still undecided, they don't take the next step to scheduling a call or purchase.

The Larger Market Formula

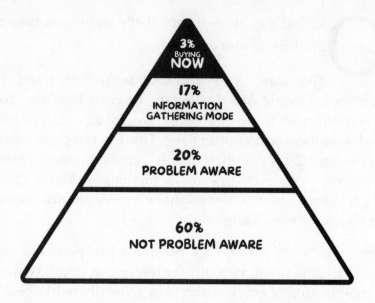

Obviously, these people have a need or problem they're looking to solve; otherwise, they wouldn't have opted-in for your HVCO in the first place. However, they aren't in the 3% of the pyramid that are looking to buy now.

This is where it really gets interesting. Remember I said the biggest profit opportunity online lies in the 97% of prospects who aren't in 'buy now' mode? They are the biggest market, and marketing to them can give you a *huge* advantage over your competitors. You just need to know how to treat them. They might be right on the edge of buying but just need a little something more. So, you engage The Magic Lantern Technique and send these fence-sitters a video sequence that teaches them something that ultimately moves them closer to their desired outcome.

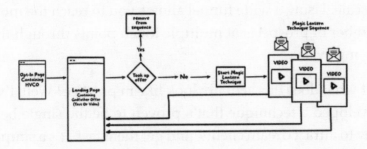

This is a series of two or three videos that give them pure value. They're not selling anything, just giving them some value in advance and taking them closer to their desired outcome. At the end of each video you include a **call to action** saying something along the lines of:

'If you liked this content and you're committed to getting X outcome, I've got a really great offer for you. I've put some time aside in my calendar to help you solve this problem or get your desired outcome. And you can go ahead and book in some time with me here'.

This may seem complicated, but the result of this video sequence is that you turn a good chunk of that disinterested 97% into genuine, eager buyers. You'll still get your standard 3% of 'itchy-to-buy' prospects from the first step of this funnel, but this next chunk is a far bigger volume of buyers and is like gravy on top. It's what will let you spend more on acquiring a customer, make more money from your ad spend, and put you miles ahead of your competition.

Using The Larger Market Formula and appealing to a broad

audience of cold traffic gives you the biggest opportunity to scale. Using a wide funnel allows you to reach the most number of prospects at multiple touch points through the buying cycle.

But what does this actually look like in practice? Well, I've developed a technique that's proven to be the single best way to attract dream clients, and get them fast. It's a simple step-by-step approach that works to simultaneously create desire and trust in the market place, and genuinely build goodwill that helps your prospects whether or not they buy from you.

The Magic Lantern Technique is like guiding your prospects down a metaphorical path to their desired end state. Along the way, you provide a ton of value and all the goodwill that comes with it.

So, at this stage, you've created your HVCO and you've got people bobbing around in a sea of other people raising their hands and saying, 'Yeah, I'm interested in what you're selling'. Here's where the Magic Lantern Technique comes in and provides further value to those people to get them to book in an appointment with you or take the next step towards becoming a paying client or customer.

Remember, we live in a day and age where scepticism is rampant. People are more cynical now than any other time in history. It's never been harder to convince a prospect that what you're selling works and that they should do business with you.

If you think about the traditional way people market

their businesses online, it's typical to have some piece of content they give away for free, and then once the person downloads it, they just thrash them to death with a barrage of emails full of hard-sell messages.

This leaves people thinking, 'I wish I'd never given my email to that person. That wasn't an enjoyable experience at all'. We want to set ourselves apart from that, and be radical and different to what everybody else is doing in the market place.

At this stage, we know who our dream buyer is and what they look like and what their characteristics are. We've done this using the Halo Strategy and really digging into their pains and fears and hopes and dreams. And then we've created that HCVO which specifically targets that dream buyer, and now we want to really think about where they are at.

Let's put ourselves in their shoes and think about where they want to go. What does your dream buyer's desired *end state* look like?

I'll use a PR consultant to illustrate how we can go through this process and implement The Magic Lantern Technique for that kind of business.

We start by thinking about where this person is right now. Where are they in their journey?

- Draw out a timeline.

- On one end of the timeline, draw your prospect.

- One the other end, draw a symbol that represents their desired outcome.

- Map out 4 or 5 milestones necessary for your prospect to reach their desired outcome.

- Think about your prospect as if they were someone you want to do incredibly right by (that's how you should be thinking about your customers in any case!).

- Create a piece of content that gives them a result.

- Create another piece of content that gives them another result.

- Create another piece of content that gives them another result.

- As we give them their advanced results, we move them closer to their desired outcome, and simultaneously build goodwill and trust, whilst reducing scepticism.

The Magic Lantern Technique

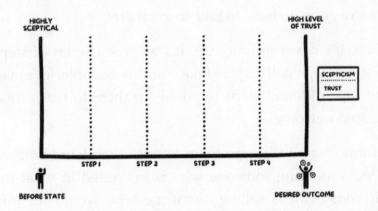

Let's say our PR consultant's dream buyer is a person (or organisation) who wants press coverage but isn't getting any. No one knows about them. They don't have any logos to add to their website or credibility touch points, and they haven't been mentioned in the press. They're totally unknown. So we ask ourselves, where does this person want to go? What does their desired end state look like?

If I hazard a guess, it would be someplace where they're getting lots of press, right? They would be really happy if they were featured in all the top blogs and being interviewed on podcasts. They're on *Forbes* and *Entrepreneur*.com, and lots of different business and media sites. There's buzz happening around their brand. They're getting attention and press. Everyone knows about them. They've got logos to add to their website. And so that's where they want to go – it's their desired end outcome.

So, The PR consultant has used a High-Value Content

Offer to target their dream buyer - people who *want to get press*. They've identified where they are and where they want to go. The next step is to map out the required steps they're going to have to take to get there.

Note, it's never in one leap; it's always a series of steps that someone will need to take. For this example, let's map out four different steps required for them to reach their desired outcome.

At this stage, we've got them to raise their hand with an HVCO as being someone who is interested in what the PR consultant is selling. Someone who would identify with and download an HVCO is someone who is in a less desirable 'before' state and wants the benefits promised by the HVCO.

We're going to provide them some value *in advance* that's really going to take them, one step at a time, closer to where they want to go.

Step One

Create a piece of content around a 12-step social media audit. This could be a checklist, a PDF, or a swipe file – whatever you prefer.

Typically, I find video content really powerful, and you don't need to get all fancy with the production; you can just shoot it with your iPhone. It's the value of the content in the video, not the quality of the video, that's most important.

In this instance, let's create a checklist that our dream buyer can use to audit their own social media presence. They can use it to make sure that from the point of view of a social media presence, their affairs are in order. In this way, if a journalist or influencer were to check them out and do a bit of digging around, they'd be sure that everything looked just the way it should, and they came across as a credible business deserving of attention.

So, that's what we're going to give them! This will allow them to go ahead and implement it, and then start seeing some results; or at the very least, they'll start feeling good about themselves because they're now moving towards where they want to be.

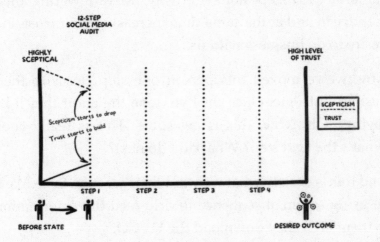

Taking this person from where they are right now, we've moved them one step closer to where they want to go, and throughout this process we've increased trust and reduced scepticism. As I've mentioned, scepticism is rampant, and that's largely caused by the internet, as it's dramatically lowered the barriers to entry for businesses and 'experts' to get out there and start marketing themselves. Thus, there are a lot of people with a website or blog who are touting themselves as 'experts'.

Understand that once your prospect has downloaded your High-Value Content Offer, they'll still have a high level of scepticism at this point. It would have lowered a little bit, because you've provided them some value, but it's still high. Throughout this process we're trying to lower that scepticism whilst simultaneously increasing our status as an authority in this space and building trust, so they believe what we're saying. When we start this process, you can see that the scepticism is high, and as we provide value at each step along the way, we're lowering their scepticism and at the same time increasing their trust and desire to do business with us.

Now we've moved this person one step closer to their desired outcome. Once they've done the audit they'll be saying, 'Oh, wow, this is awesome. This is really cool. What's the next step? What do I do next?'

And this is exactly what we want their reaction to be. We'll be using an email sequence to drip feed this information to them after they download the HVCO.

So what does that next step look like, and how do we really get them one step closer towards getting the press coverage they desire?

Step Two

Now let's put together a video called 'The 11 Things Never to Say to a Social Influencer'. Bang! Now we're moving!

They will be reaching out to influencers and starting to try and get featured in blogs and other platforms.

You can position it like this:

'You know that influencers are constantly getting pitched by start-ups and businesses that want to be featured on blogs and all that kind of stuff; they're getting hammered all the time, and these are the things that they hate. This is how they hate to be spoken to. This is how everybody approaches them, and these are the things that you never want to say to them'.

So, we're not saying at this stage, 'This is what you should say', we're saying, 'This is what you <u>don't</u> want to say'. We're providing value, letting them know how the PR business works and giving them some ideas they probably would never have thought of. Basically, we're making them more informed and moving them further down that line.

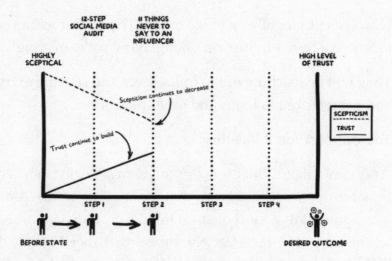

Again, what we've done is move them one step closer to their desired outcome, and as we do that again, the scepticism is going down as we continue to provide more value, trust levels and desire increase. Do you see how this is really radically different from what everyone else is doing?

Now, stop and think about the person going through this process.

At this point they've downloaded your HVCO. You've hit them with a cool and valuable piece of information. They've done an audit for their social media channels. Then you've given them a video that tells them the things not to say to an influencer, and they're like, 'Wow, this is just awesome! This person (you) just provided me all this value, and they haven't even tried to sell me anything. They're literally just dishing out value, without asking me for anything'.

Ok, let's keep moving! The way these videos are designed is that 80% is value and content and 20% is a pitch at the end where you say:

'If you're enjoying this content and this whole process, then you'll want to know that I've put some time aside on my calendar for you to schedule a call', and simply insert your Godfather Offer here.

If you're a PR consultant, your Godfather Offer might be a 12-Month PR Blitz Blueprint of exactly what you can offer. You might also add in what those press milestones would look like over the next 12 months in a calendar format.

We're using our Godfather Offer like an ethical bribe to invite people to speak with us. And what happens next is almost magical!

Instead of cold-calling or begging your friends and colleagues for referrals, you'll have people reaching out to you and booking in on your calendar… all robotically and automated!

You can use a service like Calendly or ScheduleOnce where you can prefill your availability and block out times that you're unavailable. And let me tell you, these are the hottest leads that you will ever get.

Because all you've done is provided value to them, and you've already proven that you're unlike everybody else, so their scepticism has already decreased. So they're going to reach out to you and book in a time on your calendar when they're ready, willing, and able to do business with you.

Usually when someone downloads a piece of content online, they then start receiving calls, with people hammering them with the hard sell, asking them to buy straight away.

They're doing the equivalent of walking into a bar and asking someone to marry them straight up cold. But not us, no. This process is radically different from that.

Let's keep rolling.

At this stage we've provided them with two valuable pieces of content and they're moving towards their outcome. Let them sit for a day or two at each step, making them really hungry for that next piece of content. Remember, you always want to hint in your emails that there's something else coming.

Like, *'You thought this was great, wait till you see what I've got to show you in the next two to three days'*. This makes them eager to open up all your emails and see what treasure is inside.

Usually when you get an email from someone that's marketing related, you delete it, often without even opening it. However, with The Magic Lantern Technique you're making people eager to receive your emails, and that's a very, very powerful thing.

At this stage we think, 'Okay. What's the next step we need to implement to move them one step closer to where they want to go?

Step Three

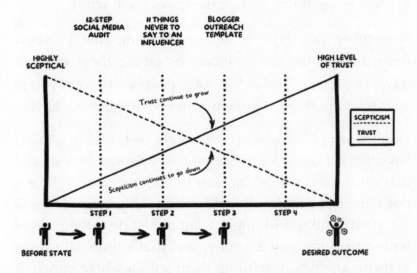

We've already told them 'The 11 Things Not to Say to an Influencer'. A great next step at this stage might be an outreach template to pitch influencers. We can dress that up and make it really sexy, something like, 'Our Five-Step System for Getting Featured on *Tech Crunch*, *Entrepreneur*, and *Forbes* in 30 Days or Less', and give them an outreach template they can use to contact influences and start getting featured on blogs.

Again, we've moved our prospect one step closer to their desired outcome and by doing this we've also lowered their scepticism and simultaneously increased their trust and desire to do business with us.

At this stage our prospect is saying, 'Shut up and take my money!' This really is a strategy to get prospects banging down your door to do business with you. Making them jump through all types of hoops and even refusing to sell to them straight out of the gate drives them wild!

Remember, our goal is to keep moving that prospect towards their desired end state by giving them value in advance for free. And at this stage people will want you to start pitching them… But we won't be doing this just yet.

Don't worry, I know what you might be thinking… *'Wow, Sabri, I'm not just going to give out all my services for free'*, and that's not what I'm asking you to do. Yes, there will be a percentage of people who go through this process and will get great results, and might want to just do it themselves without paying you a penny, and that's fine! All power to them. You'll be providing them with a whole bunch of value, and that's going to happen in any case, right?

But right now, today, not everybody who contacts you or asks for a proposal buys from you, right? Of course not, because in marketing we're only ever counting on a very small subset of the market to actually take the desired action we want them to. Whether that's clicking on an ad, coming through to our landing page and converting into a lead or sale, booking an appointment, or a prospect becoming a paying client. It's always going to be a small percentage of people who actually do that thing you want them to do.

That's how business works, and it's what we count on as marketers. With all the people who *don't* do what we want to do, typically, everyone else is just hammering these guys with the usual horse shit – Buy! Buy! Buy! Cold hard sales messages, over and over again.

They're not building any value in their marketplace. By going through this process, we're increasing the total percentage of people taking the desired action we want them to, which is the end game and results in mucho dinero in your pocket.

And when I say it increases the amount of people that buy, I mean it *dramatically* increases sales!

Because this process is the easiest way I have ever discovered to become a master of persuasion, this simple approach will make you one of the most persuasive people on the planet, no matter what field you're in. This is the 'master secret' of knowing how to persuade almost anyone to do almost anything.

Remember, because you're going through this whole process, all the people who don't buy straight away are going to stay on your list. They're not going to unsubscribe because of all the value you've provided, and you'll create a lot of brand equity, trust, value, and goodwill within your marketplace, which is just so different to how everybody else is marketing themselves; and when you do that, they might not be ready to buy right now, but when they are ready, who do you think they're going to go to? You!

In addition, the customers you really want are not going to have the time to do all this, right? Even though you're giving them all the tools, they're not going to have four hours a day to work on the public relations for their business. At this stage, we're just proving to them that we can really help them, whether it's today or tomorrow.

By giving them real value in advance, we reduce their scepticism and increase their trust and desire to work with us.

So let's take a look at where we are. They've raised their hand with a HVCO, then they've downloaded the 12-Step Social Media Audit from there, then we've hit them with the video of 'The 11 Things Never to Say to an Influencer'. They've gone through and gobbled up that content.

Then, after we've told them what not to say, we've actually given them a blogger outreach template, which they can use straight away to reach out to influencers at *Forbes* and *Tech Crunch* or wherever they want to get featured. By this stage, they might have received some results and said to themselves, 'This is just incredible. This is so cool! I'm getting all this value. Their strategies work. I believe this person can indeed help me!' Their scepticism is almost gone – and then we offer them one more piece of value.

It's important that all of these steps feed into the big picture. You don't want to be talking about an outreach template before they've got these other things in order. It's a gradual progression to get them to that desired end outcome. You don't want to lead with the biggest thing that's closest to their desired outcome, because that doesn't make sense in the chronological order of the steps.

The Press Release Template

The next action is to accelerate their results and pump them up on steroids by giving them a *press release template*. This allows them to go out and really blow things up and thread in any of those credibility points from the blogs they've been mentioned in, which is going to increase the likelihood of this press release really catching wildfire and getting traction. So again, we've moved them one step closer to their desired outcome.

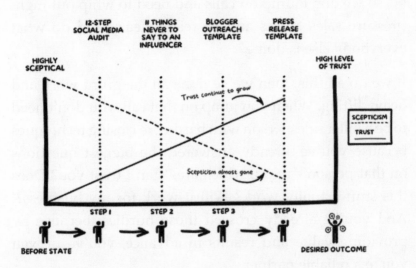

They're really, really close to getting the desired outcome they really want, and throughout this whole exercise their scepticism has pretty much evaporated and their levels of trust are sky-high.

They trust in our strategies and in us as the authority expert; the scepticism has been removed, thus the friction between you and making a sale has eroded.

Let's not forget, your goal through this is to not only create goodwill and trust, but to also generate leads and make sales. If you're in the business of selling a service for a fee, the end goal is to get people on the phone. Because we know in order to get paying clients, we're going to have to jump onto the phone and speak to people, and we want to make sure that by that point, their scepticism is as low as it can possibly be. And we want to make sure that their trust and desire to work with us is as high as it can possibly be, so we don't jump on calls and need to whip out high-pressure sales tactics and be really sleazy and do what everybody else is doing.

If we do all this, then we've done all the grunt work and heavy lifting. When you jump on that call, you don't need to be a killer salesperson with hard-core closing techniques because you've already answered the biggest questions on that person's mind, which are, 'Can I trust you? Does this stuff actually work? Will it work for my business?' And you've already crossed those hurdles, because by providing value and results in advance, you've proven you're a reliable partner.

You've picked up your magic lantern and taken them down the path, and at the end of that path is their desired outcome, the one they've been searching for. You've illuminated the way throughout that process and proved to them that you can help.

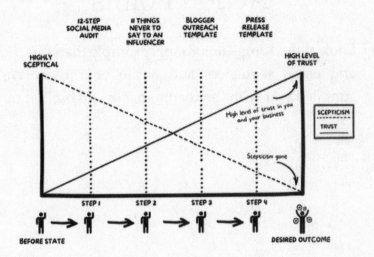

I can't stress it enough; this is the most powerful approach to generating itchy-to-buy leads that create an avalanche of sales for your business. It's like nothing you've seen before, and it will almost instantly position you as a trusted authority in your marketplace.

If you've ever wondered how to generate more piping hot leads than you could ever imagine – this is it! You'll be jumping on these calls and there will already be a relationship. They'll feel like they know you because they've watched all these videos and accepted your free information.

It's a proven and predictable way to get your prospects calling you at the moment they're ready, willing, and able to give you their cash!

They feel like they've got a connection with you, and all the resistance that's typical on a sales call has been removed because you've already answered many of their key questions.

Action Points

- Look at the King Kong funnel example that uses video and email sequences and create your own. We've supplied you with the roadmap, now go build it out.

PHASE 7:

Sales Conversion

Now that you've generated a list of leads by getting prospects to raise their hands and say they're interested in what you're selling (we know this because they've downloaded your HVCO), and motivated them with your Godfather Offer to ask for help in an ethical way (a way that genuinely helps them instead of being based on hype and pressure), the last step is the **sales mechanism.**

The job of the sales mechanism is to make a sale. Whether you're delivering your sales pitch over the phone, face-to-face, at a seminar, or through a webinar, everything leading up to this point has brought you here, and now it's time to close the deal.

If you're selling a service, the best way to close the sale is to have a free 30, 45, or 60 minute zero-pressure, very helpful sales conversation. This conversation can close 80% or better, depending on your own individual results.

Sell Like A Doctor

Throughout my sales career I have read over a thousand books and made over one million sales calls - so I've learned a lot from my work in the trenches.

But the biggest breakthrough I had about selling came from the most unsuspecting place of all… *Doctors!* That's right, it was only after I learned to 'sell like a doctor' that my sales truly exploded beyond all belief!

What do I mean by 'sell like a doctor'?

I've found that 90% of salespeople get it wrong. They basically vomit every feature and benefit of their service during their sales presentation in the hope that something hits a nerve that will make the prospect buy.

This is the equivalent of having an appointment with a doctor where they poke all your body parts while asking, 'Does that hurt?' and 'How about here?'

Instead, a good doctor begins by asking, 'Where is the pain?'

Remember that in the medical profession…

A prescription without a diagnosis is malpractice

And it's the same in sales.

Once you've got a prospect raising their hand to identify themselves as interested in what you're selling, and you have them motivated to schedule a call to speak with you using The Godfather Strategy, *only then* is it time for you to make the diagnosis.

Because you must understand, even when you use the advanced selling system outlined in this book to qualify leads, there will always be a percentage of prospects who won't be a great fit for what you're selling.

Selling is about taking your prospects from a less desirable 'before' state to a more desirable 'after' state, and if what you're selling doesn't deliver your prospect to their ultimate desired outcome, then – to put it simply – *don't sell to them!*

Imagine you walked into a doctor's appointment and they prescribed you medication before even asking what brought you in.

You walk in there and the first thing that the doctor says is, 'Hey, I've got these new antibiotics that just came in. They're really good and I think they can really help you out. I'll write you a script now because you definitely need them'.

Naturally, the first thing you're going to say is, 'Wait – why do I need antibiotics? I have even told you my symptoms'.

Such a doctor would have their licence taken away from them and likely be thrown in jail.

Now, if you sell the wrong thing to a customer the consequences won't be as harsh, but you will have problems on your hands very quickly.

You don't want to get onto a sales call with a prospect and have a preconceived attachment to selling someone a particular product or service. While that may be your ultimate goal, starting out with 'selling' in mind is the wrong approach.

That's just like the doctor thinking the next person who walks in the door is going to need these brand new antibiotics.

You want to have your attachment on an **accurate diagnosis of the problem.**

Think about when you walk into a doctor's office. A good doctor will have all of his or her attention on giving an absolutely spot-on diagnosis.

That's what makes a good doctor and it's what makes a good salesperson. You have all of your attention on the diagnosis, not the prescription.

As a salesperson, you're trying to diagnose someone's issue and then, *if what you're selling can help them,* you make them an irresistible offer – an offer they can't refuse.

If you can't help them, shoot them straight and let them know that what you've got isn't a great fit and won't help them solve their issue.

Not only is it the right thing to do, but it also creates goodwill in your market if prospects understand you're not simply quick to make a sale, but are genuinely trying to help them solve their problems.

The word will get out and you will be rewarded for this approach.

To add to this, by doing the diagnosis before you start talking about 'what you got', the words that come out of your mouth will be more powerful – because they'll be tailored to the symptoms and issues your prospect has just told you they're experiencing.

Practical Application

First, let's walk through a scenario where you've had a prospect respond to your Godfather Offer and reach out to schedule a time to speak with you.

In order for them to take you up on your offer, you want to make it compulsory that they fill out a short survey before doing so. Nothing too intrusive, but it should give you more insights into the problem they're trying to solve, where they are in their journey to solve it, and where they want to go (their goals).

This survey and application process gives you critical information to determine whether you can help this person and if you are a good fit for what they're trying to achieve. It also changes the psychology of the sale, as they are reaching out to you and asking for your help.

So they've filled in your survey and answered your questions, and they've qualified themselves to you, jumping through hoops to speak with you. Therefore, there's never, ever, ever any cold-calling, or any 'typical' sales calls involved.

The conversion process needs to be more about eliminating the stuff they have done or are currently doing that isn't working, rather than about the features, bells, and whistles of what they're going to get from doing business with you.

Don't go into great detail about your service/program/training: that's what your prospect is buying. Your objective is to give them an idea of how their life could be better by working with you.

For most of us, it's very tempting to talk about our services, our coaching, or our expertise, but the problem is this only translates into you talking more about you than about solving their problems. And they didn't book in this call to hear about how great you are. They booked the call because they have a problem they are motivated to solve. They couldn't care less about you.

Everyone's favourite person is themselves, and their motivation to schedule a call, like it or not, is completely self-serving.

Finding Your Prospect's 'Why?'

It's incredibly important that you find the real reason they booked in this call with you.

What is their 'Why?'

You pick up their call and ask:

'Hello, Mike. Please tell me your biggest motivation for taking the time out of your busy day and scheduling this call with me.'

Or the short version:

'Hello, Mike. How may I help you?'

And then you shut up and listen. If you get the real reason and not some fluff like, 'I just wanted to see what you have to offer', then great. If not, you'll need to dig deeper.

Once you get their true deepest desire, dig even deeper by asking opened ended questions:

- 'Okay, can you tell me more about that? What do you mean? What exactly are you referring to when you say _____?'

- 'Why do you believe you're experiencing this?'

- 'Okay, so why is _____ important to you?'

- 'Why are you serious about _____ right now?'

- 'What have you done previously to try and fix this?'

- 'How long has this been going on?'

- 'What has prompted you to look at this now?'

- 'What isn't working, and why do you think it isn't?'

- 'Why do you feel you haven't achieved this yet?'

After you've shone a light on their problem and then kicked their bruised knee (some of them may not have known how big their problem was until you highlighted and agitated it), they're now primed for you to help them solve their burning problem.

They have a 'bleeding neck', meaning they have an immediate problem for which they need a solution, and they're ready to go to the hospital in just about any vehicle you can provide.

Where Do They Want To Go?

Get your prospect to tell you about where they want to go and their desired outcome. Then find out their 'why', and get them to picture exactly what life will be like after they get there.

One way we do this is by saying:

'Mike, if we were having this conversation twelve months from today and you were looking back at the past twelve months, what would have needed to happen for you to be happy with your results?'

I learned that question, by the way, from a book called The Dan Sullivan Question. Here are some variations:

- 'Mike, what are you looking to achieve in the next 12 months? What would that do for you?'

- 'Where do you want to be?'

- 'What do you want to achieve?'

- 'What revenue do you want your business to be doing?'

- 'What would that do for your lifestyle?'

- 'How much do you want to weigh?' (If you're selling a weight loss programme)

- 'How much money do you want to be making?' (Financial advice)

- 'What would you like your relationship with your spouse look like?'(Relationship advice)

Get an answer to these questions, let them tell you exactly all the things they're trying to achieve, and get some specifics before moving forward with the call.

More questions (and remember, you're going to listen and pay attention to the answers!):

- 'I understand – and what is your motivation for achieving X?'

- 'How would these change things for your business/life if you achieved X?'

- 'Okay, so when you make more money/lose more weight/connect on a deeper level with your spouse/ have more time... what difference is that going to make in your life? What's the reason you want to do this?'

It's important you get a temperature check on exactly what they want to achieve and why. Then help them to paint a vivid picture of what this exactly would *feel* like.

The Admission

This is where you get your prospect to express everything they've been doing so far. How they've struggled. All their frustrations. Get all their challenges out. What has worked. What hasn't. And why.

Get them to admit that everything they've tried simply isn't working, and they need a proven system and roadmap from someone who's done it with success. Get them to admit they've had enough of doing it by themselves and want help.

- 'Why is this important for you to figure out and get it working?'

- 'Okay, on a scale of one to ten – one being not really important and ten being extremely important – how important is this for you to do?'

- 'What does it mean if it doesn't get done... what does that represent/what does that look like?'

- 'Okay, so what you're telling me is what you're currently doing is not working, right? And it sounds like it's time to finally do something about it?'

Remember this: If it's not important to them, then politely end the call. If they don't have a burning desire to solve this problem, it doesn't matter what you're offering or what you're charging, they won't buy.

Delivering Value

After you've established the burning problem they're trying to solve, this is the part of the call where you transition into the value you promised up front in your Godfather Offer.

Once we've asked all our questions and got all their answers, we simply help them formulate a plan based on their answers. Genius, I know.

Once we find out where they are and where they want to be, and we've gone through all these questions, and got all the stuff we can get from them, all the 'raw materials' so to speak, we now build them a bridge to get there in the form of a plan.

- 'Ok Mike, I can definitely help with that. Would you like me to show you a little of how we could do that and what would be involved?'

This is an incredibly important part of the call and is where all sales pitches generally fall short. You want to prove to your prospect that you can help them by actually helping them. Not simply agitating a problem, or telling them what you do and how much you charge.

You might be thinking, why would we want to help them solve some of their burning problem now, instead of straight up selling them our solution? Well, because scepticism is so rampant, people are so dubious and so untrusting in what people say they can do for them. They want to *see it!*

And rightfully so. The internet is plagued with 'experts' selling them pixie dust, unicorns, fairy tales, silver bullets, and magic pills to achieve their desired outcome overnight. There are legions of novices who quickly slap on the guru cap and try to sell their untested and unproven solutions. Ignore this and you'll fight a losing battle. You must be neither in the dark nor in denial as to what you're up against.

A way to kill this scepticism is to prove to them that you can help them *by actually helping them.*

Remember, no one likes to be sold, but everyone likes to buy. You want to get your prospects excited by solving a part of their problem on the call, or at least making it very clear you can help them solve it and leave them begging for more.

It's like when you go to a fancy restaurant, and the waiter brings you a delicious hors d'oeuvre – you know, one of those little appetisers or small starter dishes. You eat it, it's incredibly tasty, and then your digestive juices start going crazy and you order half the menu!

It's the same principle here. You want to leave your prospect starving for the main course, which is your core offer.

Ultimately, you want to leave your prospects better than when you found them. Meaning, regardless of whether or not they choose to buy, you want to deliver massive value and create goodwill.

Remember, your prospects have likely been told everything you're telling them before, but they've never achieved the results they wanted. By following this process and delivering value you prove that you are different from everybody else by giving them some value in advance.

How you do this: Splinter off a tiny part of your offering and deliver it then and there on the call. Hash out a problem and then demonstrate how you could help them solve that.

EXAMPLE: If you're a PR consultant, you could show them a site like HARO (Help A Reporter Out) that helps them connect with hundreds of journalists who are actively looking for experts and businesses to feature and weigh in on articles. Also, let them know there is a lot that goes into managing this and how to get the best traction.

EXAMPLE: You might be a digital marketing consultant. If so, you could show them how much search traffic certain keywords are getting on Google, or where their competitors are getting traffic from, and for how much, using sites like SEMrush or SimilarWeb.

EXAMPLE: If you're a financial planner, you could show them how to offset their income tax by setting up a family trust. Or use a credit check service/software on the call to see if they could get a better mortgage rate on their home.

Get creative and think about unique ways you could deliver value and show them live on the call that you can help them by actually helping them. This strategy is almost like magic, and makes people buy with as little resistance as possible.

Getting The Commitment

Once you've delivered your value piece it's now time to gain commitment.

IMPORTANT: If you've identified on the call that the prospect is not a good fit, politely let them know; and even if they want to buy, do not sell to them. It will simply cause you more headaches in the long run and will drain you. Additionally, you can't build a business based off working with clients who aren't a great fit.

If they are a great fit, this is where you gain commitment and segue into your offering:

- 'Ok, Mike, how did you enjoy that?'

- 'Does that sound like the type of help you're looking for? Would you like to know more of the specifics?'

- 'Ok, Mike, it looks you would be a great fit for my program or service. Do you want to hear how that works?'

The Prescription

This section of the conversation is to simply tell them what you've got to offer and what your program can help them achieve. Tailor this to the specific problems they told you they were having earlier in the call and position it as exactly what they need – because it is!

Notice this is the first time in the call that you start talking about what you have to offer. Nowhere at any point during our conversation have we told this person what to do. Instead, now we're going to start prescribing solutions to help them on their way to their desired outcome.

We'll say something like this:

- 'Based on what you've told me, it sounds like this would be a great fit to help get you [thing they want] and [other thing they want]'.

Now simply list out everything they will be getting in your services or program.

You may have to write out this section of your script because everybody's service and offer is different. Write it out, read it aloud, and ensure it rolls off the tongue; and then practice saying it over and over again to get the delivery perfect. This is crucial.

This overview should be no more than two minutes long. Don't waffle on and on, and work yourself into a frenzy where you are just rattling off every bell and whistle your service includes.

Be prepared and get used to delivering this overview and applying it specifically to each prospect's pains, fears, hopes, dreams, and desires to make the prospect feel your offering is exactly the answer they've been looking for. Use the same words they use to describe their problems and goals.

Provide the features and then finish with how these translate into benefits for them. Do not harp on about all the technical bells and whistles of your offering. Instead, focus on how it will help them solve the issue or problem they're looking to solve. Focus on the end result, not the process.

EXAMPLE: You'll have predictability in your business, more time, more money, less stress, greater freedom, increased security.

EXAMPLE: You'll have more energy, feel great, and be able to fit into that old pair of jeans you love.

The Close

Based on the prospect's tone and involvement in the call, you should have a good read if they're 'cold', 'warm', or 'hot'. However, we still want to do a temperature check and test close by asking the following:

- 'Mike, I want you to understand this is not for everybody. It does take time and commitment from yourself, and requires that you actually do the work and take action. With that said, why are you serious about solving/achieving_____right now?'

- 'Before I move forward, Mike, to the financial investment, I'd like to first know something from you. After hearing about what is available, the benefits you'll receive, and how this is going to get you closer to achieving your goals, and getting you the help that you're looking for, do you have any other questions or concerns that I haven't covered?'

- 'Okay, you're clear and comfortable with everything thus far, and you know how everything works? Okay, great'.

- 'Other than money, is there any other reason that it wouldn't make sense to go ahead and get started today?'

- 'Okay, if the money makes sense, then we can get you set up and reaching your goals immediately!'

- 'Ok Mike, based on what we've discussed, why do you feel you would be a good candidate for this program?'

This question is powerful. It turns the tables and gets the prospect to start selling themselves on why they would be a good fit for you and why they feel they would be successful.

State your price and what your services cost. Say it with pride and conviction. *Do not hesitate* for a second and do not pause to get a confirmation once you state your price. This is a run-on sentence, and you want to go on to further explain the pricing.

All packages should have a set-up fee. This is for two reasons: 1) to offset your customer acquisition costs, and 2) to create urgency using a Fast Action Bonus (FAB).

Fast Action Bonus – Going back and forth costs you time, energy, and money. Let them know you can drop the set-up fee if they make a decision now.

As a backup you, can give them 24 hours if they truly need to speak with their partner.

- 'Well, Mike, as I mentioned, there's normally a $1,000 set-up fee. However, I've found that people who are able to make decisions quickly always turn out to be my best clients. This is because they're decisive and can take action. Also, going back and forth costs me time, energy, and money. So for that reason, if we can get this all sorted for you on the call today, I'll waive the $1,000 set-up cost off your investment, making it just the $___. How does this sound Mike? Can we go ahead and get this set up for you?'

THEN, YOU DON'T SAY ANOTHER WORD.

There's an old saying in sales: 'The person who speaks first, loses.' You've stated your offer. Now you must show confidence by waiting for their response.

You're looking for confirmation on moving forward.

You wait for Mike to say,

- 'How does that work?'

- 'What are the next steps?'

- 'Yes, let's do it!'

- 'Ok, how can we pay?'

- 'What is the process to getting signed up?' Then you say,

- 'Ok, great! We take Visa, MasterCard or Amex. Which card would you like to use today?'

Collect their payment details and boom! You've closed the deal and won a client!

Now you might be thinking, 'It can't be that simple'. But it is.

This is the complete opposite approach to what most people use when making sales. Typically, they follow the 'guru-centric' model where they've worked to put themselves up onto pedestals so they could be admired, appreciated, and respected enough to be purchased from. Instead we use this process to create massive relevance for your clients by being able to solve their biggest and most burning problems.

Recap: When selling coaching, consulting, or professional services, it's important to weed out people quickly if they aren't going to be a good fit. You do this by using surveys and applications. That way, it frees up more time for you to spend with people who are a good fit and that you can actually help.

The survey and application pages allow you to pre-frame your prospects by having them jump through hoops, qualifying themselves and confirming they are a good fit. When the fate of your business is on the line – which it always is because sales is the oxygen for any business – you need a proven 'rinse and repeat' process and script for converting leads into sales. You don't want to have it all in your head or 'wing it'. You *must* have a script that you refine and strengthen over time.

Then when you hire people, they can follow your proven script, leaving little to chance.

But what happens to the people who go through our funnel and don't take the desired action we want them to? Which, I will add, will always be the majority of people, because in marketing, we only ever count on a very small percentage of people actually doing what we want them to do. Do we just accept this and move on to simply just generating more traffic?

No!

We nurture these people over time. We provide value and build a relationship by using email.

In the following pages I'll go in-depth on the topic of email marketing and how I've used it to generate tens of millions of dollars in sales.

PHASE 8:

Automate And Multiply

My Secret Weapon to Turning any Traffic Source into My Own Personal Honeypot of Hyper-Profitable Endless Sales

If you had to strip me down naked, take everything I've got, and leave me with nothing except for *one* marketing weapon of choice, what do you think it would it be?

My contacts? JV partnerships? Google rankings? My ability to turn ice-cold traffic on Facebook into profit?

Nope! I would choose *email!*

Why? Email outperforms every other marketing channel. Period. And one of the biggest mistakes I see businesses make *is not building an email list from day one.*

Email is the bedrock of my business today. It's by far my #1 source of revenue. It's how I communicate with my community, launch new services, and reach my customers. Email is the engine that's generated millions of dollars for my business — more than every other channel we've used *combined.* And it's not just our business that depends on email.

It turns out that having an email list has a forty-fold impact on your bottom line. Yes, you read that right. According to a 2014 study by McKinsey and Company, for every dollar you put into email marketing you get back forty dollars more than you would through Facebook, Instagram, and almost every other marketing channel. Forty times more revenue!

And according to the Direct Marketing Association (DMA), for every $1 marketers spend on email, the average ROI is $44.

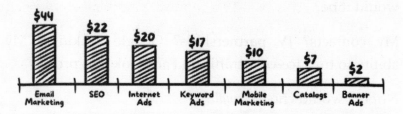

ROI PER $1 SPENT

| $44 | $22 | $20 | $17 | $10 | $7 | $2 |
| Email Marketing | SEO | Internet Ads | Keyword Ads | Mobile Marketing | Catalogs | Banner Ads |

Don't make the mistake of not building this incredible asset for your own business. Email delivers more leads than any other marketing channel, and 42% of businesses have listed email marketing *as the top digital marketing channel for lead generation.* So if you're serious about business growth, an email list is critical.

I get asked all the time about why am I so bullish on email? Aside from the obvious case as seen in the statistics above, my reason is simple: it's a huge risk to build a business on a platform *owned by somebody else.*

While everyone's freaking out about Facebook messenger bots and screaming from the rooftops, 'email is dead', Facebook can change its policies overnight – which they do all the time.

Google can penalise your site and flatline your traffic.

But *you own* your email list. Nobody can take it away. The moral of the story is this: don't leave the fate of your business in somebody else's hands. If you build your audience on some external platform, you're at their mercy. And you're not in control.

In addition to this, email is incredibly efficient... It can sell to 10 people as easily as it can to 100,000 people. In other words... *it scales!* You can write just one great email message and profit from it again and again.

Just like this one email I wrote in 30 minutes that has already made me $467,163:

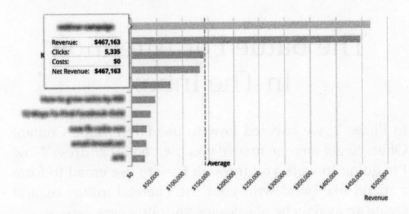

I wrote this great email once, and thanks to the power of email marketing and automation, it's been a workhorse that keeps working, grinding it out and bringing in money – without me having to exert any further effort.

When I look at sales and marketing, I look to create automatic and robotic-like selling systems where you can write an email, shoot a video, write a sales page, or record a webinar, and then profit from it again and again on autopilot.

Over 117,391 people have read that email in the last two years. All automatically, robotically. I didn't lift a finger.

Email is really one of the biggest levers in your business, and hopefully by now you see why it's so important.

So if it's that important, what do you think you should spend time getting good at? Yes! Email.

Now I'm going to pull back the curtain and show you exactly how to write throat-grabbing emails that get people to buy.

The Battle For Attention In The Inbox

In Phase 2, we covered how to use High Value Content Offers to get anyone to give you their email address. Now I'm going to walk you through how to use email to form a friend-like bond with your list, channel influence, and create an avalanche of sales for your business.

We're going to talk about what you do once you've got a list of prospects.

When it comes to email, there really are only three things that matter:

- Get it delivered

- Get it opened

- Get it clicked

And we're going to cover everything in this chapter.

Step 1: Get It Delivered

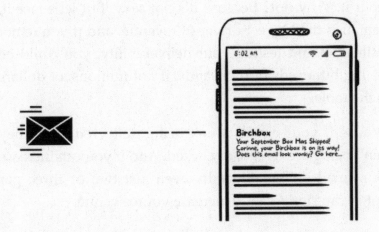

When most people think about email marketing, they think, 'All I have to do is get an email service provider, upload my list to a piece of email marketing software, click the send button, and they'll handle the rest.'

It really doesn't work that way. You have to really work to ensure your emails get delivered. Considering the smart filtering systems of today's mailboxes and email providers, achieving a high inbox deliverability rate is not easy.

In today's day and age, email deliverability is determined by three things:

- Sender reputation.

- Bounce and complaint rates.

- Recipient engagement.

For businesses that are serious about growth, email deliverability is arguably one of the most important metrics. However, you won't find any marketers talking about it. Why not? Because it's not sexy. But let's face it, if email is the biggest driver of revenue, and if you're not optimising and testing your deliverability, you could be leaving hundreds of thousands, if not millions, of dollars on the table.

Because if your emails aren't being delivered, then they aren't being seen, read, or clicked. And if you can increase your email deliverability by even just two or three per cent, it can significantly increase your revenue.

So, while this is going to get a little technical, stay with me because I promise it will be worth it.

The Platform

The very first step to getting your email delivered is to be on a good *platform*. What platform is best? This all comes down to the size of your list (how many people are on your list) and the economics (how much it will cost you to send out to that list).

A great place to start if you have a smaller sized list (sub 10,000) is MailChimp, which has some of the best deliverability in the industry. However, it can prove to be relatively more expensive as your list gets bigger.

Some other good platforms are ActiveCampaign, GetResponse, AWeber, and Drip.

Without getting too technical, each platform does better with different email providers. Depending on your list size, you might want to use multiple platforms for different email providers, or you might choose a platform with the best deliverability for the majority of your list's email providers.

Primary Email Providers

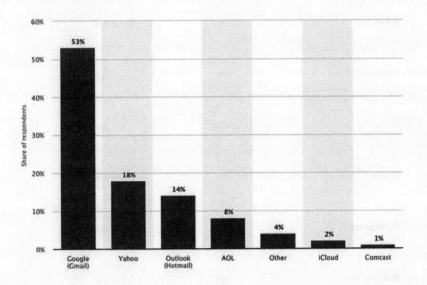

Email Deliverability

PROVIDER	DELIVERABILITY RESULT %	OVERALL RATING*
ActiveCampaign	96	★★★★★
Constant Contact	93	★★★★★
Drip	89.8	★★★★★
MailerLite	89	★★★★★
ConvertKit	88	★★★★★
MailChimp	82.6	★★★★★
Aweber	79.8	★★★★★
GetResponse	78	★★★★★
Benchmark	75.8	★★★★★
SendinBlue	75.6	★★★★★

Deliverability by Email Provider

PROVIDER	GMAIL PRIMARY %	GMAIL PROMO %	YAHOO %	MICROSOFT %	AOL %
ActiveCampaign	100	0	100	100	100
GetResponse	100	0	97.5	11	100
MailerLite	100	0	100	100	100
MailChimp	0	100	100	40	100
SendinBlue	100	0	100	13	100
Benchmark	100	0	100	0	80
Aweber	100	0	100	19	100
Constant Contact	100	0	100	100	100
Drip	100	0	100	100	100
ConvertKit	100	0	100	83	100

It's clear that some email platforms are better at delivering emails than others, and specifically at getting through to certain email providers like Microsoft.

I strongly believe that deliverability should be an important factor to consider when choosing an email software service. And while it might seem like I'm deep in the weeds here talking about highly technical elements, it's important to fully understand the profound effect that deliverability plays in driving sales. The results aren't linear – they compound and exponentially move the needle for your sales:

Small Hinges Swing Big Doors

More delivered > More opened > More clicked > More see your offer > More buy $$$

Sender Reputation

Just like a credit score, your IP address (the unique string of numbers that identify your computer) has a reputation called a *sender score*.

If you're like me, your eager little brain is probably saying, I wonder what my sender score is?

Well, you can go to www.senderscore.org and find out for yourself.

This website is run by a company called Return Path, and it will tell you what your reputation and sender score is. Anything above 90 is good, anything above 95 is great, and you shouldn't be having any deliverability issues. However, it is something you need to frequently check, as you want to uncover any issues sooner rather than later.

If you score anything below 90, you have some issues that need to be corrected. Here's a list of the most important metrics that affect your sender score and reputation.

The Most Important Metrics That Affect Sender Reputation

- **Message is read** – A positive indicator that the recipient wants to receive your emails.

- **Message is replied to** – A positive indicator that the message is desired and presents a personal interest to the recipient.

- **Message is forwarded** – A positive indicator that the recipient finds the message valuable and thinks that others should see it too.

- **Message is marked as 'not spam'** – A very strong positive indicator that email providers use to train their spam filters.

- **Message is moved to a folder** – An indication that the recipient wants your email, but also wants to better organise it and access it later.

- **Sender/domain is added to the address book** – A positive signal indicating that the recipient wants your emails and wants to make sure your future messages will be delivered to their inbox.

- **Message is deleted without being opened** – A negative signal that your email is of no interest to the recipient.

- **Message is marked as spam** – A very strong negative signal that your email is unwanted and not worthy of being in their inbox.

Creating Goodwill With Your List

The single most important strategy for increasing your sender score is by sending more engaging and valuable emails. Don't just send your list promos and offers. You need to create goodwill with your audience and have them hanging for your next email, which is why the Magic Lantern Technique works so well.

An easy way to manage this is to make sure two thirds of your emails are content and value, and one third is offers and promos.

This rule is not hard and fast. In your content pieces, you can make offers. Throw them in the P.S. and ensure the main body of the email stands alone as a valuable piece of content.

Warm Up Your New IP Address

After you select which platform is best for you and you've got a new IP, it's important to start sending slowly with a low email volume to establish an IP address reputation. Over time, you can increase the volume.

Formatting and Styling

Contrary to popular advice, your email shouldn't look 'beautiful', with heavy images and sexy graphics. Why not? Firstly, who do you think send these types of heavy emails with lots of images – individuals or businesses with commercial intent? Businesses! These types of emails send a signal to email providers that the nature of your email isn't personal, and therefore it hurts deliverability. And if it doesn't get delivered, nobody's opening it, and if nobody's opening it – you guessed it – *nobody will be buying!*

Secondly, while you may think, 'But it looks so schmick and sexy', know that in the case of email, schmick and sexy doesn't drive sales. It's been proven in countless split tests. However, most businesses keep overdesigning emails and attempting to make them look 'beautiful'.

Logos in the Header

A lot of business owners and even seasoned marketers put their logo at the top of each email, and then have padding around the email with fancy buttons, almost styling it up like a web page.

These heavy-weight emails kill your deliverability, because who sends these types of emails? Businesses! And what types of emails do businesses send out? Promotions! And therefore, this type of email gives a signal to the email providers that this is a promotion, and so they will either stick it in Gmail's promotions tab or throttle the deliverability. This not only kills the amount of emails that arrive in the inbox but also hurts consumption of the email, which we'll cover in the following points.

This is the bottom line: If you're serious about email marketing and want to run world-class email campaigns, you must have a robust infrastructure providing accurate email authentication, high sender score, clean sending IP address, and a good sender domain/email reputation.

It sounds like a lot of work – and it is! However, it's well worth the effort when the sales come pouring in.

Switch Up the Sender

Sending out emails from multiple people within your company or organisation improves open rates, and therefore has a cascade effect on sender scores and reputation overall improving your deliverability.

Such as: james@hotwaffles.com, susie@hotwaffles.com, david@hotwaffles.com.

Step 2: Getting It Opened

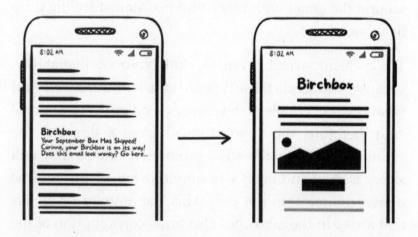

What was the subject line for the highest opened and highest earning email in history?

'Hey'.

Who sent it?

President Barack Obama.

Really, it's true. It was that casual, straightforward, and highly 'unprofessional' greeting coming from the man who commanded arguably the most powerful office in the world. Straight from the head honcho who was (at the time) the president of the United States. So that explains a huge part of its success. I mean, honestly... How often do you get an email from the president, just saying 'Hey'? And the better question is, who wouldn't open it?

That wasn't the only unusual email that played an integral role in Obama winning re-election. Other subject lines included, 'Join me for dinner?' 'It's officially over', 'It doesn't have to be this way', or just 'Wow'.

All very personal, and they relied heavily on curiosity and intrigue to get the open. The Obama campaign raised $690 million online. The majority of it came from the fundraising emails that peppered inboxes for a two-year period. They employed a team of 20 writers and a sophisticated analytics system to measure and improve their effectiveness.

The campaign would test multiple drafts and subject lines – often as many as 18 variations – before picking a winner to send out to tens of millions of subscribers.

The lessons from Obama's master email marketing campaigns aren't just a recipe for politics or making money, but for winning eyeballs in the brutal death match to grab your attention in the inbox.

Compare that to all those commercial messages, coupons, and sales emails you get. How many of those do you open?

One out of every ten? Or worse, do they just sit and rot in your spam folder?

What's the difference? And how can you write emails that always get opened? That's what we're covering in this section.

Think about your email inbox for a moment. When you fire it up for the first time every day, what do you do?

Check, check, check, check, check... *Delete!*

You delete everything that appears to be promotional or commercial and that you know is safe to delete. Why is it safe to delete those emails?

Because you know, from reading them in the past, that they are promotional, commercial, and generally speaking, a complete waste of your time.

Based on years of experience, it's my contention that everybody scans their inbox categorising emails into two distinct groups:

A 'P' group and a 'C' group.

The 'P' group contains emails that are, or appear to be personal. Like emails from friends, relatives, colleagues, business associates, and so on.

On the other hand, the 'C' group contains those emails that obviously contain a promotional or commercial message.

Now, here's the way it works: Everybody always opens all of their 'P' group emails. This is for obvious reasons, as everybody wants to read their personal emails and doesn't want to miss a bit of news or a question from a friend or family member.

What happens to the 'C' group emails? Do they always get opened? No, they don't. Most of the time they get archived or deleted immediately without ever being opened – that is, if they've survived today's sophisticated spam filters.

Sometimes, if it looks interesting enough, 'C' group emails will be left inside the inbox to read 'later'. And, of course, sometimes, if the email subject line looks interesting enough, or if the person receiving it has some spare time, is bored, and has nothing else to do but mindlessly hang around in their inbox, then, maybe, just maybe, the 'C' group emails will be opened.

That's the reality, my friend.

Obviously, people aren't going to buy from you unless they read your emails and see your offer. And they can't read your email and see your offer unless they open it.

And so, as we begin to craft our email, what is our first objective? You are indeed right! Our first objective is to get our emails into the 'P' group.

How do we do this? We first have to make the email look personal. (Or at the very least ensure it doesn't look commercial.)

This starts with the sender's name and the subject line.

Emails that you want to get opened should *always* come from an email that appears to be personal.

That means no 'sales@letmesellyou.com'.

Or if you are going to be using such an email address, at least change the sender name associated with the email address to yours or a member of your team, i.e., 'Bryan Miles'.

The idea is that it doesn't get 'selected' and thrown into the 'C' group and deleted before it's even opened!

How to Get Anybody to Open Your Emails

The next step in reaching our objective is getting our emails not only *not deleted but opened.* And no, we're not going to cover some ninja subject line email hacks or scripts that force your emails to be opened.

I'm going to show you the single most important element to get anybody to open your emails.

Every media, whether it's Facebook, Google Ads, or email, comes with *context.* Typically speaking, when it comes to email, nobody wants to be emailed a commercial message from a business. They only want to hear from their friends. Your task, then, is to sound as much like their trusted friend, colleague, or family member... *without using trickery* or *being gimmicky... or* worse, *lame.*

Because if you screw this up, you'll lose their trust and your emails will never be opened again. And as result, over time you'll develop a bad sender score, and even worse... *email blindness.*

Email blindness is when someone's email is there in your inbox, but you've mentally written them off as a waste of time. You've probably opened two or three of their emails in the past and have gotten no real value from them or they bored you to death. So, over time you don't even see those emails anymore when you scan your list. They become invisible.

The chances are good that your emails are likely causing email blindness for your readers. How can you tell? Well, are you happy with your open rates?

Every time you send out an email, are you flooded with sales and eager to buy leads? Or are your open rates, sales, and click-through rates not where you want them to be?

If it's the latter, you're causing email blindness. And there is only one cure to the money-murdering disease that is email blindness and that is to write emails that *entertain*, *excite* and *engage* your readers.

The number one thing I fear when I send out an email is that it will be boring.

People live boring lives. They are constantly scrolling through Facebook and Instagram wanting to be entertained and inspired. They have ordinary friends, with ordinary jobs and ordinary routines.

They are bored!

Don't add to this by writing limp, boring and dull emails that put your readers to sleep.

Be that person in their life who brings them some spice, some entertainment and excitement to their dull vanilla lives. Do not be boring.

Make it so every time your readers see your name pop up

in their inbox, they get a tiny little hit of dopamine in their brain that makes them want to read your emails.

Do this and they will be hanging out for your next email, looking forward to receiving it; and when they do see your name appear in their inbox, they'll almost stumble over themselves in a rush to see what you have to say... and to get a hit of that dopamine.

This becomes a positive anchor towards you, your name, and your business.

Once you've cured email blindness, here's what happens:

Your open rates will sky-rocket. When you ask them to click a link, they click a link. Your readers will follow you religiously on whatever adventure you choose to take them on. (But it better be entertaining!)

If you master this, like *really* master this, you will create an email selling machine that drags in not thousands or hundreds of thousands or millions or even tens of millions of dollars; but rather, email copy that has the potential of increasing sales for you (or your clients) that can add up to hundreds of millions of dollars.

But this doesn't happen by accident. It takes effort, and most people have no idea how to secure this kind of relationship and friend-like bond.

The takeaway being, nothing will increase the amount of sales your emails bring in more than writing exciting and entertaining copy that spices up the dull life of your readers.

We'll cover more of how exactly to do just that later.

How to Almost Force People to Open Your Emails with Your Subject Lines

It's no secret that one of the primary drivers of email open rates is your subject line. Other than the sender name, it's the element of an email that usually stands out the most in your reader's inbox.

We've battled hard to ensure maximum inbox deliverability with our sender scores and reputation, and now is the time to practically force our readers to open up our email once it's arrived.

There's lots of advice out there to help you write better subject lines. And most of this advice has a lot in common. It's mostly about subject line 'hacks' and formulas, i.e., 'Use emojis in your subject lines, or use this magic email subject line formula, blah, blah, blah...'

Instead of these 'hacks', I like to focus on the strategy more than the tactics. And my primary objective with anything to do with email is to do everything in my power to ensure my emails end up in the 'P' group. And therefore, the prime objective when writing subject lines is that they appear to be personal.

Stop reading right now and take a look at your inbox. Go ahead. I'll wait.

What did you see?

Let me guess.... You saw all, or most of, the following:

- Emails from your friends / family.

- Emails from colleagues.

- Alerts and updates from social media sites, e.g., 'Dave wants to join your network'.

- Emails from your manager or senior executive.

- Emails from businesses and blogs.

- Bills and electronic statements.

- Software and tool notifications and update.

Some emails require an action. Others don't.

Some emails have to be stored for your records, while others don't.

Some of those emails you dread having to deal with. Others are easy.

But all of these categories of emails fall into two distinct groups. You guessed it, the good ol' 'P' and 'C' groups.

And you can bet your bottom dollar the ones assured to get opened and actioned are the emails that appear to be personal.

Therefore: Your email subject line's primary objective is to sound as much like their trusted friend, family member, or colleague as you can... without being tricky or gimmicky or lame.

The more you sound like a friend, the less you'll scream, 'I belong in the "C" group! Delete me!'

Here are the subject lines of a few personal and work-related emails in my inbox:

- crazy check this out

- can I chat to you about this in morning?

- let's buy this for Melia

- Friday's playgroup

- Bali accommodation options

- approval needed

What do those subject lines all have in common?

They:

- Use lower-case or sentence case – not Title Case or, even worse, ALL CAPS.

- Lack almost all punctuation.

- Keep it to four or five words, max.

- Ask questions.

- Tell you enough to want to open them, but not the whole story.

When crafting your email subject lines, you need be doing all of the above, in order to make your subject lines look personal and in the 'P' group.

If you sit down to write your email and find yourself struggling to come up with something, a great place to look for a bit of inspiration is at Native Advertising. You can see examples of Native ads at www.aol.com. Once you get there, scroll down the page a little until you see this:

Notice the 'AdChoices' link on the top right and bottom left. These are native ads served up by an ad network called Taboola. These headlines can be a good source of inspiration.

Intrigue is a proven winner to draw in readers. But when using this style of clickbait-y subject lines, you have to close the loop in the email. The subject line creates burning intrigue and curiosity and the email needs to satisfy it. This shows your readers that you can deliver, and that you're not simply tricking them to open your emails; this makes them more likely to take action and keep opening up your emails in the future.

If you still can't come up with anything, then there are templates and formulas. However, as a general rule I'm not a fan because everyone uses them and they can come across as generic if you're not careful.

I mean how many times have you seen '7 secrets to losing weight' or '10 ways to make more money'?

Subject lines like this work a few times, but after a while, seeing the same old recycled subject line formulas just gets old. It trains your readers not to engage with them and causes email blindness.

That's why I personally try to avoid formulaic subject lines.

But let's get real. Sometimes you need a template or formula to fall back on when your creative juices aren't flowing. They can help you get unstuck or help you get you started with some fresh ideas.

So, as a last resort you can swipe and deploy this list of email subject line formulas or use them to get your creative juices flowing:

- how to make {subject} that will {benefit}

- 21+ ways to grow your {subject}

- do you think you can {benefit}?

- The only way to achieve {desirable thing} without doing {undesirable thing}

- 5 reasons why you should {subject}

- {benefit} while you sleep

- [template] 10 best {subject}

- how {name/company} does {subject}

- {name/company} can afford any {subject}, he uses {solution}

- how {name/company} got {number/desirable outcome} in {number of days}

- real {audience} use {solution}

- discover the {solution}

- {subject}, {subject}, and {unrelated subject}?

- stop {undesirable current state} now

- copy and paste these {subject} [last chance]

- discover the {solution} that will change your life today

Subject Line Length

Most email subject lines are between 41 and 50 characters. This is what I call the **'death zone'**. Why? Because everything average is wrong, and research shows this is the *least* effective character length for email subject lines. These subject lines are often crafted by 'email marketers' who are trying to cram as much info into 50 characters as possible.

According to data from Return Path, 65 characters seems to be a sweet spot for email subject lines, which is about 15 characters more than the average subject line. When subject lines are 61-70 characters long, they tend to get read. However, I've personally found the best success from selling millions through email, is that wherever possible, short and personal get the best results.

For subject lines, from 1 to 20 characters is where the magic happens.

My own findings are backed up by recent research from Yes Lifecycle Marketing. Their research also concluded that emails with shorter subject lines tend to get significantly higher open rates and click rates.

The report was based on data from more than seven billion emails sent in the second quarter of 2017 by Yes Lifecycle Marketing clients in a wide range of industries.

They too found that emails with subject lines between 1 and 20 characters in length have the highest average open rate (18.5%), unique click rate (2.4%), and click-to-open rate (12.9%).

Compared with medium-length subject lines (21-60 characters), *longer* subject lines (61+ characters) have slightly higher average open rates, unique click rates, and click-to-open rates.

Subject Line Character Count	Proportion of All Emails	Open Rate	Unique Click Rate	Click-to-Open Rate
1 to 20	5%	18.5%	2.4%	12.9%
21 to 60	74%	13.8%	1.2%	8.5%
61 and over	21%	14.8%	1.3%	8.9%

In summary: Test short and sweet subject lines against super long subject lines and see where you have the most success. But whatever you do, don't get caught up in between, in the death zone.

Assess the Terrain

Inboxes are busy and crowded places. Most of your audience is on multiple lists. Your direct competitors. Non-direct competitors. The works.

In order to write emails that get opened, you should know how your emails stack up and stand out against those you're battling against for your reader's attention.

Sign up for every email and/or newsletter from people in your industry. See what these people are sending out, how frequently they're emailing, what their subject lines are, what type of content and CTAs they're using in their emails.

That's right: You need to see every email your competitors are sending.

Then start what's called an 'email swipe file', which I recommend you divide into folders in Gmail, Outlook, or whatever you use. This allows you to take a panoramic view of the market and the landscape you're fighting for attention in.

Look, even though the subject line is one of the shortest elements of your email, it's the one part you should be willing to spend the most time on. It's the key to sucking people into your email. Get it wrong and almost everything else doesn't matter. Get it right and watch sales go through the roof.

Preheader Text That Burns With Intrigue

The preheader is the short summary text that follows the subject line when an email is viewed in the inbox. Many mobile, desktop, and web email clients use preheader text to give the reader a preview of the email's content before they open it. Here's an example in Gmail:

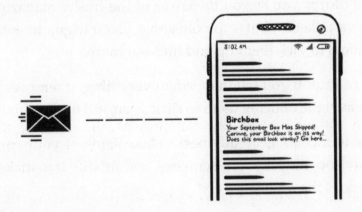

Preheader text is what I call the 'sniff test' used by subscribers as a pre-screening tool along with the subject line, because it's the second thing a subscriber sees when they get your email.

It's these two elements they use to decide whether or not this email belongs to the 'P' group or the 'C' group, and whether or not they should open your email.

As we've already covered, if your emails don't get opened it's impossible to get people to click-through and take your desired conversion action, like making a purchase or an enquiry.

People are time-poor and looking for any excuse to deem

your email irrelevant so they can delete it. Preheader text makes it easy for them to do this without even clicking into the email.

This means the copy here must be on point. The key with preheader text is *not to tell the whole story* and to have it *burning with intrigue*. Think of this section as the headlines and blurbs you see on the cover of the trashy magazines we've talked about – the ones that use intrigue to entice readers to pick them up and find out more.

Be careful. If you tell the reader everything, it removes all the intrigue enticing them to click open and find out more.

I've found it's generally best to take some of your email body copy, ideally mid-sentence, and modify it to make it work as the preheader text.

It's also great to use a 'cliff-hanger' or the 'open loop' copywriting technique where you leave the reader wanting more.

A cliff-hanger is a scene in a movie, book, newspaper story, or TV show that *holds something back* from the reader or viewer.

The promise is that if you keep reading or watching, you'll eventually be rewarded with what you want to know.

Suspense and intrigue are the main ingredients of a good cliff-hanger.

Using curiosity as the hook in preheader text keeps things sort of vague, yet gives the reader just enough to make them want to know more. Nothing is more effective for raw clicking power.

Examples:

- 'Man showers in lemon juice, you won't believe what happens next. Find out here >>'

- 'Leading cardiologist says carbs are not the problem (this is)'

- 'I walked into my manager's office and said these 3 simple words...'

- 'Cat comes face-to-face with a rhino and both creatures' instincts just take over'.

With that said, you don't have to use pure suspense or intrigue to create a great cliff-hanger. There are other approaches including:

- Humour

- Amazement

- Doubt

- Challenges

And while the most effective cliff-hangers are unique and personal to you and your audience, you can also think of cliff-hangers as common phrases like these:

- For example

- Let me explain

- Here's what I mean

- Here's why

- Sound silly? It's not

- Case in point

- This is how

If you can't think of a unique and personal cliff-hanger, then go with one of the above. Using preheader text in your emails will get you more opens, more clicks, and more sales!

Email Timing: The Best Day to Send Email

According to research by CoSchedule, for maximum inbox deliverability and open rates, you should prioritise your send days in this order:

- **Tuesday**: This is hands down the #1 best day to send emails, according to the majority of the data from these studies.

- **Thursday:** If you send two emails a week, choose Thursday for your second day.

- **Wednesday:** While no single study showed that Wednesday was the most popular, it came in second place several times.

The Best Time to Send Email

CoSchedule found that while many of the studies returned varying results, here's how you can prioritise your send times based on data:

- **10 am:** While late-morning send times were the most popular in general, several concluded the best time to send emails is at 10am Another notable time is 11am.

- **8 pm-midnight:** I bet you didn't expect that one. It looks like emails generally receive more opens and clicks later in the evening. This is likely due to people checking their email before going to bed.

- **2 pm:** It looks like you might be successful by sending your emails later in the day as people are checking out of work mode or looking for distractions.

- **6 am:** This makes complete sense given that research from the Center for Creative Leadership shows that 50% of you begin your day by emailing in bed. Bingo! Before you even stand up, you're opening emails. Good morning!

The Winners Are...

This list combines the *best days* with the *best time of day* to send out emails, in descending order:

- Tuesday at 10 am

- Thursday at 8 pm

- Wednesday at 2 pm

- Tuesday at 6 am

- Thursday at 10 am

- Wednesday at 8 pm

- Tuesday at 2 pm

- Thursday at 6 am

- Wednesday at 10 am

- Tuesday at 8 pm

- Thursday at 2 pm

- Wednesday 6 am

Test Everything!

Everyone is wrong until proven otherwise – that's my motto. With this said, you'll need to test these days and times against your own list. Send out your emails at the best days and times as suggested above. Then analyse the data from your tests to see when you got not only the best open rates, but also the most traffic and conversions.

Step 3: Getting It Clicked

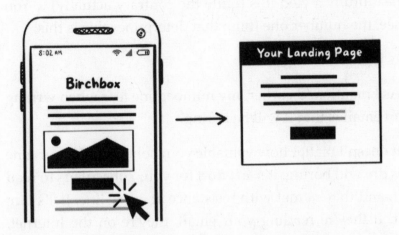

Ok, now it's time to whip your emails into shape. In this is section we'll dive into the anatomy of high converting emails. What works and what doesn't. Step-by-step, you'll learn how write and design emails that actually make you money.

First up, *tone is everything*. Unlike a classic novel, where you know what tone to expect, writing for email is different. It's much more personal and conversational. People are really good at detecting if pieces of writing on the Internet – be they emails, blog posts, Facebook updates or tweets, Google ads, YouTube comment threads – are meant for them or not. And the key signal is how you put the words together. The tone tells you a lot about whether an email is worth your attention or not. And it's your tone that will help people answer their eternal question – 'In an inbox of infinite options, should I read this email?'

The number one thing that determines this is not your grammar. It's not the length of your email, or how beautifully styled it is (quite the contrary actually) …You see, the number one thing that determines this is this:

Is it entertaining?

As I mentioned earlier, my number one fear when writing an email is that it will be boring.

It doesn't matter how valuable your content is. If your tone is dry and boring, it's an effort for your subscribers to read it, and they're met with resistance at every line. Let's face it: If they're reading your email, they're on the Internet, meaning they're just two clicks away from super-models in bikinis on Instagram, funny cat videos, or what their friends are up to on Facebook.

Therefore, your emails must entertain! Don't write limp, boring, dull emails that lull your readers into a coma.

Be that adventurous person in their life who brings them some spice, entertainment, and excitement to their vanilla existence.

Be controversial, funny, and exciting. Hit them with that 'happy shot', make them smile and want to read your emails.

I don't care if your market consists of lawyers, financial planners, neuroscientists, architects, or a member of the royal family... they will never be 'bored into buying'. They will only respond to passion and entertainment. Passion, entertainment, and showmanship are the missing ingredients in copy and advertising today.

In today's digital age, everybody seems to be more concerned about offending a few losers than they are about selling to a multitude of winners.

Whom will I offend? Who will unsubscribe from my list? Will I be stoned in the streets? Who the hell cares about that small percentage of cowards who have nothing but time on their hands, people who will hide behind their keyboards and write scathing comments in response to almost every solicitation they receive?

I know I certainly don't. But I see countless companies give up millions of dollars in sales every year just so they won't offend a small percentage of complainers who'll never buy from them anyway.

Listen: When you write email copy, you should never lie, never cheat, never use poor taste, never use trickery, never be crass, and never insult your reader's intelligence.

However, you absolutely must stop watering down your copy, playing it safe, and making it lifeless, boring, and lacking in passion, all in the hopes of not offending those who'll never do business with you anyway.

Instead you must entertain, excite, and spark passion in your readers. Be polarising. This will enable you to form a friend-like bond with your audience by being 'real' and levelling with them and not trying to be some uptight prude.

And don't just talk about business. Tell them about your personal life, what you got up to on the weekend, what you do for fun, about your crazy ex-mother-in-law who's like a fire-breathing Godzilla. Let them see your blemishes. Engage in casual banter like you do with friends. Tell them stories and then, and only then, hit them with your valuable ideas, strategies, and tactics on how to help them achieve their desired outcome.

As a result, like me, you'll get countless emails just like the one below, in this instance the subscriber had completely forgotten how he got on my list:

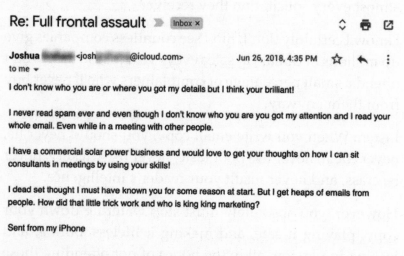

Re: Full frontal assault » Inbox ×

Joshua [redacted] <josh[redacted]@icloud.com>   Jun 26, 2018, 4:35 PM
to me ▾

I don't know who you are or where you got my details but I think your brilliant!

I never read spam ever and even though I don't know who you are you got my attention and I read your whole email. Even while in a meeting with other people.

I have a commercial solar power business and would love to get your thoughts on how I can sit consultants in meetings by using your skills!

I dead set thought I must have known you for some reason at start. But I get heaps of emails from people. How did that little trick work and who is king king marketing?

Sent from my iPhone

This email is just one example of many.

I've personally sold millions and millions of dollars' worth of goods and services through email. And it's one of the most powerful, most highly leveraged tool for business growth that exists.

Anatomy of a High-Converting Email

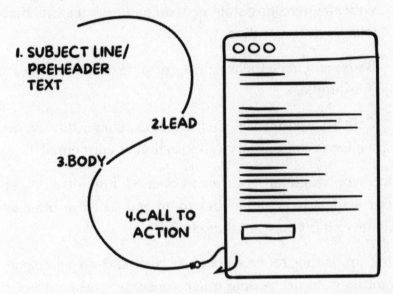

Every element of your email has one primary goal: to get the reader to take the next step. Every line of copy should keep their eyes glued to their screen, sliding down the slippery slope.

Your reader starts at the top of the slope, reading the subject line, and then immediately slipping down to the preheader text, and then they open your email and slide into the opening line of your copy and then immediately slip down to the next line, slipping to the next line and so on and so forth.

In this sequence:

- **Subject line/Preheader**: Grabs your reader by the throat and forces them to keep reading. After reading your subject line, their brain should be burning with intrigue to find out more.

- **Lead:** Drag them into your copy by captivating them with an interesting statement or 'pattern interrupt' that jolts them to attention.

- **Body:** Fascinate them with a gripping or unusual story or example.

- **Call To Action:** Get them to click, share, buy or do whatever the primary call to action of your email is.

Once you've gotten your email opened, how do you get your readers to actually click to go and see your offer or whatever it is you want them to do?

First up, if they're ever going to click and do what you want them to do, people must 'consume' and read your email. The very first element of this is design.

1. Email design: how your email looks is as important as what it says!

While your email subject line is one of the primary ways to get email opened, the *design* of your email is how you get it *read*.

As I mentioned previously, you might think that beautifully designed emails with lots of images, animated-buttons and a HTML-enhanced responsive theme would increase the amount of people that read your emails and then click. But this couldn't be further from the truth.

Don't believe me? Let's take a look. When you quickly scan this email, what's the first thing that comes to your mind?

Ok, stop. Let me guess. Immediately you knew it was from a business. You knew it had commercial intent. Therefore immediately it goes into the 'C' group of emails. Consequently, you knew it wasn't important or didn't require an action from you, and then you deleted it.

What's the very first thing that tipped you off? Let me guess – it was probably the subject line with each and every word capitalised (when was the last time a friend sent you an email with letter case in the subject line?) Then, once we do open it, there's a logo at the top in the header. Your friends would never send you an email with the logo in the header, so don't do it. Instead, put your logo in the signature.

This is not just common sense. It's backed up by research and data. Digital marketing behemoth HubSpot researched the idea of HTML versus plain text emails. To summarise their findings, they too found that HTML emails actually decreased both their open and clickthrough rates.

Aside from proper list segmentation, nothing boosts opens and clicks as well as an old school, plain-text email.

Why? It's simple. Plain text emails look more authentic and less commercial than HTML-enhanced emails. In addition, email filters are smart enough to weed out over-enhanced emails from plain text emails – so it helps with your deliverability too.

People see email as a one-to-one communication tool, and when was the last time you got a beautifully designed HTML-enhanced email from a friend about something important? Simple plain text emails seem to reflect the personal nature of email, while HTML-enhanced emails scream 'commercial mass marketing'.

Check out this example from an email I received about business lending:

This is the perfect example of what *not* to do. It's completely over designed, there's no copy, and the images are completely unrelated. I'm sure the creator would be saying to their manager, 'How great does this email look?' Unfortunately for them, the design and polish of your emails doesn't make people trip over themselves to buy, in fact, it does quite the opposite.

No one wants to feel like you're marketing to them. They'd rather feel like they've opted in to receive information that will help them reach their desired outcome. Email is a way to get your list to know, like, and trust you, which is the number one way you convert subscribers into paying customers.

Takeaway: Send plain text emails rather than HTML-enhanced emails.

2. Talk to them like a friend

So, how do you cut through, get noticed, and eventually sell to your list? First up, write conversationally and don't try to sell them straight out of the gate. Instead, just get your message read first. The only way to do that is to get your emails in the cherished 'P' group by being more personal.

Just write like you would to a friend. It's just fine to start an email with 'Hey there'. Let people into your lives a bit, show them your personality, as quirky as it might be.

This is the opposite to how most companies write emails. Their writing screams, 'I'm trying to sell you!'

Use short sentences and write the way you talk. Good email copywriting is not super-dense technical stuff. The last thing you want is an overwhelming wall of text when someone opens your email. You want your emails to look approachable. Lots of small paragraphs, or even better, single lines of copy – just like the example below:

Gmail

Grown men weeping
1 message

Sabri Suby ▓▓▓▓▓▓▓▓▓▓▓▓   Thu, Jul 20, 2017 at 2:46 P

Happy Thursday Sabri.

No, I'm not talking about the outrageously entertaining Conor McGregor and Floyd Mayweather press conferences that took place last week.

Today, I'm writing to you with a very important question…

One that could have your business profit immensely.

Do you know what is the most brutally competitive market in the world online?

A market where a mere miss click or tap on AdWords ad could set you back $195…for a SINGLE CLICK!

A game where the stakes are so high…

The competition so fierce…

It makes grown men weep…

What industry am I talking about?

INSURANCE

Insurance companies spend more on digital marketing than any other industry, and because of this, they are plagued by:

- The highest average Cost Per Clicks
- The fiercest competition on SEO
- Tough regulations on what you can and can't say
- And ever increasing competition across all channels

So what does all this have to do with your business?…

How can you profit from this madness??

Well, what better place to look for inspiration on tactical strategies to grow your business than the most fiercely competitive landscape on planet earth?

Where else better a place to analyse what the top players are doing with digital marketing to choke out their competition and make them 'tap out'.

Nowhere!

And in the spirit of providing value to you, regardless of whether or not you're a client, or ever become one…

We've put together a shocking case study that proves just how fiercely competitive digital marketing is for the $500 million insurance company iSelect.

It's hot off the press and you can read it here to find out what all the fuss is about.

Be amazing,

Sabri

Sabri Suby
Founder & Head Of Growth

KING KONG ▓▓▓▓▓▓▓▓
▓▓▓▓▓▓▓▓
▓▓▓▓▓▓▓▓

P.s. if you would like to know how to utilise some of these growth strategies to dramatically increase your traffic, leads and sales - we've still got a few FREE $1,000 digital marketing consults left for the month, you can grab one here before they're booked up.

A good test is to read everything you write aloud. Make sure everything reads smoothly. Great emails feel like a conversation between you and your best friend.

While you want to give your readers a glimpse into your life, remember, ultimately your readers *don't care about you or what you do.* They only care about themselves and *what you can do for them.* The tone, your stories, and everything is else must be geared to make the content engaging and entertaining. The bottom line is, all of your email copy should focus on your reader's needs and wants.

3. Study the herd and do the opposite

Think of the landscape and context in which the reader will read your email. Will it be seen — or ignored — in a sea of other emails vying for their attention?

How can you make them pick you? Look at the promotions tab or spam folder of your inbox right now. Most of the emails you'll find there will be doing the exact same thing. The subject lines will be the same length, the same casing, the same kind of tone – maybe even the same emojis in the subject line. If other people are going long, then go short. Study what the other people your readers are subscribed to are doing – and do the opposite.

4. Make it visceral: bring your email copy to life with specifics

Vague copy is a one-way ticket to inflicting email blindness on your reader. Take a look at the simple edits you can make to turn vague copy into specific copy. Notice how much more powerful the specific copy is:

Boring: 'Increase your sales'

Specific: 'Stop for a moment and imagine what it would feel like to double your sales in the next 90 days… profits would skyrocket… you'd be able to increase your bonus… you'd feel secure that your business was on sound footing and you wouldn't have to spend the weekends worrying about work anymore… you'd finally be able to 'switch off' and actually enjoy the fruits of your hard work'.

Boring: 'You'll lose weight and look great'.

Specific: 'You'll finally be able to fit into that sexy little black dress and turn heads wherever you go… and even be the envy of all your friends'.

Boring: 'Be your own boss'

Specific: 'Imagine breaking the shackles of your soul-sucking 9-to-5 job, killing your calendar and living life on your terms! Picture this: You wake up as the sun streams through your curtains. You don't even own an alarm clock! You roll over to check your iPhone, Facebook, and Instagram. You jump out of bed and run through your morning workout before eating a leisurely breakfast with coffee (and no this isn't the weekend – it's Tuesday!). Then you get a text from a friend who's in town… want to meet for lunch? You can do that, too — and no, you won't have to ask your boss if it's okay. Because you're your own boss! You run your own schedule and get to work when it works for you!'

Do you see how much more relatable this type of copy

is? These edits make people feel like they know you, like you're their good friend who understands them, and with whom they can laugh with and open up to. That's key to getting your emails opened and read.

5. Don't ask them to buy, click or act – tell them!

The call to action is a command. Be specific and tell them exactly what to do – don't ask them! It means using proven phrases like these...

- Go ahead and check this out now.

- Claim your spot here.

- Click here and I'll tell you what it's all about.

- Sign up here and you will discover...

This is an NLP (neuro-linguistic programming) technique called an 'embedded command', and it's used for planting a thought (state, process, experience, or action) within the mind of the reader, beneath their conscious awareness. The purpose of using embedded commands is to move your reader's mind in the direction you want it to go without seeming to be intruding or ordering in any way.

Whatever you want your reader to do, don't ask them to do it – *tell them.*

Putting It All Together

So, there you have it. You've learned the key elements and strategies you need to create great emails from scratch that will suck in sales. And you've seen how to do it in days or weeks, instead of the years and years of pain it took me.

Getting email right is the best investment you'll ever make in your business. It can be your secret weapon like it is mine.

Your Breakthrough Email Checklist:

- Make sure you use a personal sender name.

- Send your emails on Tuesdays at 10 am.

- Make your subject lines are either two to four words or super long in length. Nothing in between.

- Write preheader text that burns with intrigue

- Above all, write emails that entertain, excite, and engage your readers.

- Ask yourself when sending every email: 'Will this email get into the 'P' group or die in the 'C' group?'

- Make your emails plain text instead of visual masterpieces.

- Talk to readers as you would your best friend.

- Make your emails about your readers — not just about yourself.

- Study the herd and do the opposite.

- Make it visceral and bring your email copy to life with specifics.

- Don't ask them to buy, click or act. Tell them!

Conclusion

W e've covered a lot of ground in this book, and, as you can see, I'm deeply passionate about this stuff.

And that's because when you get all this right, and you grow your business, it makes a profound impact on every area your life. Whichever way you want to look at it, money is a big part of life, and there's no better vehicle for creating wealth than growing a business.

The life you want to create is fuelled by the business you build. And far too often the reason people start a business – money, freedom, being able to put your kids through college, pay off your parent's mortgage or give back to charitable causes – becomes a distant dream.

That's because they get stuck being a business owner and not a business builder. They basically create a job for themselves and then work for their business, not the other way around.

All the methodologies in this book are designed to help you make the transition from business owner to business builder.

A business owner is someone who gets caught up 'in the weeds'. They get stuck on the hamster wheel of activity, executing the mundane, daily tasks that 'just have to get done'.

A business builder is an entrepreneur with a strong focus on sales and marketing. Someone who looks for leverage and to delegate anything in their business that doesn't move the money needle and pull their business forward.

A business owner is someone who mistakenly believes that simply having a great product or service is enough to achieve success.

A business builder is someone who has unwavering focus on intimately understanding their market's pains, fears, hopes, dreams, and desires.

A business builder is ruthlessly committed to not only providing the most value to their marketplace but understanding that great products and services are useless unless they can effectively and persuasively communicate this value to their market.

Having a wildly successful business is the ultimate vehicle for creating the life you've always dreamed of. From a young age you've been conditioned by society, the media, and your friends and family, all of whom have slowly chipped away at your confidence and eroded the possibilities of reaching your goals and making your dreams a reality. Naysayers – who have already given up on chasing their own dreams – start to dole out advice and plant mind-viruses inside your head, which make you second-guess yourself and wonder if you can really 'have it all'. You want a great relationship with your spouse, happy kids, an abundance of money, multiple homes, and a thriving business. But society would like you to believe that success in one area results in absence in another. I'm here to tell you this is horseshit. It's a lie spread by people who don't have the courage to go out there and manifest their wildest dreams.

You can indeed have it all.

Not only is building a wildly successful business a great lever for wealth, it also makes you stronger in every area of your life.

Business is the highest form of mental mastery. The stakes are high and it takes an incredibly high degree of focus, stamina, and wherewithal to be successful.

These traits are forged from the business you build and the plateaus you have to break through to reach even greater heights, and serve you in all areas of your life, from your relationships, your fitness, and overall mental strength to solve problems.

On your journey you will face an immense amount of pressure. Pressure is a fact of life. The people who learn to relish it are the ones who become high performers. These are the people who take huge strides forward when things are going great, and knuckle down and forge ahead in life when the heat is on.

Failure is not an option for high achievers. Pressure ignites their resolve and sharpens their focus.

If you've read this far, you may well have it in you to thrive on pressure too.

If you're serious about business success, then *now is the time to commit and take action.* You must transition from business owner to business builder – and get your business working for you, and not the other way around.

Once you make this fundamental transformation, your business and life will never be the same again. Having the ability to be a business builder, and a marketer at heart, is the single greatest skill you can attain. It means you'll never go hungry and you'll always be equipped to start and build businesses to fuel the life you want.

My strategies for growing a business are centered around turning advertising into profit. I look at marketing and advertising as assets in which I invest to grow my business. Not expenses. I'm a huge advocate of mastering this skill because I know it's a variable that won't change over time. There will always be platforms looking to monetise their audience by selling advertising. It's been this way for hundreds of years. If I know how to leverage these advertising platforms and turn eyeballs into dollars, my businesses will always be sound.

Throughout this book, you've learned powerful and valuable information that when applied will change your business and your life forever. However, all the information and strategies covered in this book are worthless **if you don't take action.**

If there's one thing I want to impress upon you, it's the importance of taking action. I want you to sit down right now and write down your action items for the next 30 days – and for the next 3, 6, and 12 months. If you don't, something else will grab your attention and you'll be off looking for the next strategy, tactic, or silver bullet for your business.

I urge you to put the blinders on and execute the information in this book – and if you do, I can assure you, you will reap the rewards.

Building a successful business allows you to manifest your craziest dreams. You deserve this success and can truly have it all, despite the naysayers. I invite you on this journey and look forward to hearing of your success and how transforming your business has transformed your life.

To your success,

Sabri Suby

One Last Thing...

I would love to hear all the successful ways you find to apply my strategies to your business and life. Please send me your breakthroughs and results. Nothing makes me happier than to hear from successful students. I collect and study all kinds of success stories, large or small, financial or otherwise. When I get yours, I'll send you back a free gift or advanced training.

Be amazing,

Sabri Suby

hello@selllikecrazy.co

1300 858 250